Conter

ASSAM G K

A Unique collection of General Awareness

Diamond Power Learning

An imprint of Diamond Pocket Book Pvt. Ltd.

Latest Important Events 2019

BHARAT RATNA 2019

Bhupen Hazarika: The President, Ram Nath Kovind on January 25, 2019 conferred the 2019 Bharat Ratna Award, country's highest civilian honour, was the legendary singer-composer Bhupen Hazarika (posthumously) from Assam who died in 2011. Bharat Ratna is the highest civilian award of India that was instituted on January 2, 1954 by the order of Rajendra Prasad, the former President of India. The award was also conferred on RSS ideologue Nanaji Deshmukh (posthumously) and former president and Congress leader Pranab Mukherjee.

Ashok Chakra 2019: Lance Naik Nazir Ahmad Wani (posthumously).

BOGIBEEL BRIDGE : INDIA'S LONGEST RAIL-ROAD BRIDGE

- Bogibeel Bridge, the longest rail-cum-road bridge on Brahmaputra river, is all set to be inaugurated on December 25, 2018 by Prime Minister Narendra Modi which will facilitate faster movement of troops to Arunachal Pradesh, the country's eastern-most state that shares border with China.
- The 4.94 km-long Bogibeel Bridge is Asia's second and India's longest rail-road bridge. It is India's only fully welded bridge, with the double-decker structure comprising two railway lines on the lower deck and a three-lane road on the upper, strong enough to withstand movement of heavy military tanks.
- It will connect the south bank of the Brahmaputra river in Assam's Dibrugarh district with Silapathar in Dhemaji district, bordering Arunachal Pradesh.
- It has been built by the Hyderabad-based Navayuga Engineering Co. It is also for the first time European codes and welding standards were adhered to in the construction of a bridge in India.
- It took 21 years for the bridge to be completed. In January 1997, then-PM HD Deve Gowda had laid the foundation stone for the project, and Atal Bihari Vajpayee inaugurated the construction work for the bridge in 2002.
- The total construction cost works out to ₹ 5,900 crore and the bridge has a serviceable period of around 120 years. For the first time, European codes and welding standards have been adhered to while constructing an Indian bridge.

Jeevan Raksha Padak Winner 2018	
• Monuj Chawtal	• Raju Garh

DHOLA-SADIYA BRIDGE: INDIA'S LONGEST RIVER BRIDGE

♦ India's longest Dhola-Sadiya bridge in Assam over nine kilometres long, inaugurated on 26 may 2017 by Prime Minister Narendra Modi as his government completes three years in office.

♦ The Dhola-Sadiya bridge is being built over the Lohit river, a tributary of the Brahmaputra.

♦ In Assam, the bridge is located in Sadia, 540 kilometres from Guwahati. Its other end is in Dhola, 300 kilometres from Itanagar, the capital of Arunachal.

♦ It about 9.2 km in length - that's nearly 30 per cent longer that the famous Bandra-Worli Sealink in Mumbai.

♦ The strategic importance of the bridge for the military is huge. With the bridge, troops will be able to enter Arunachal Pradesh, which borders China, much more quickly and easily.

♦ The bridge has been designed to withstand the weight of 60-tonne battle tanks.

♦ Construction began in 2011, when the Congress governed Assam. The cost of the project is about ₹ 950 crore.

New State Symbol		
• State Flower	:	The Fox-tail orchid
• State Tree	:	The Hollong
National-Awardees From Assam: Padma Shri		
• Smt. Eli Ahmed	:	*2017*
• Shri Jitendra Nath Goswami	:	*2017*
• Shri Prafulla Govinda Baruah	:	*2018*
• Shri Arup Kumar Dutta	:	*2018*
• Ms. Joyshree Goswami Mahanta	:	*2018*
• Illias Ali	:	*2019*
• Uddhab Kumar Bharali	:	*2019*
Assam Valley Literary Award		
• Apurba Sarma	:	*2015*
• Arupa Kalita	:	*2016*
• Sananta Tanti, Yeshe Dorjee Thongchi, Dr Rita Chowdhury	:	*2017*

Sahitya Akademi Award		
♦ Kula Saikia	Akashar Chhabi Aru Anyanya Galpa *(Short Stories)*	*2015*

♦ **Jnan Pujari**	*Maghmalar Bhraman (Poetry)*	*2016*
♦ **Jayanta Modhab Bora**	*Moriahala (Novel)*	*2017*
♦ **Sananta Tanti** ♦ **Rituraj Basumatary** ♦ **Loknath Upadhyay Chapagain**	*Kailoir Dinto Amar Hobo (Poems)* *Dwngse Lama' (Short Story)* *Kino Royeu Upamaa (Short Story)*	*2018*

Bordoloi Trophy Winners		
2014	*Assam State Electricity Board*	Green Valley F.C.
2015	***Not held***	
2016	*Three Star Club*	East Bengal
2018	*Mohammedan Sporting Club*	Oil India

Important Events

2018

- Government of India and Asian Development Bank (ADB) have signed a loan agreement of $60 million for financing project for renovation, protection and community-based flood risk management activities along the Brahmaputra river in Assam
- United Nations International Children's Emergency Fund (UNICEF) has appointed popular singer Nahid Afrin (17) of Assam as the first 'Youth Advocate' of the northeastern region to fight for child rights. UNICEF engages 'Youth Advocates' to harness their voice as agents of change in society. Nahid had made her playback debut in 2016 Bollywood film 'Akira' starring Sonakshi Sinha in the lead. She received best female playback singer award at the Assam state Film Award 2018.
- Assamese movie 'Village Rockstars' was selected as India's official entry to the Oscars 2019 (91st Academy Awards) under Foreign Language Film category.
- Inland Waterways Authority of India (IWAI) in collaboration with Assam Government has launched new Roll on-Roll off (Ro-Ro) facility connecting Neamati to Manjuli Island in Assam
- Union Cabinet approves New National Institutes Of Design,in Jorhat, Assam.
- The Digital North East Vision 2022 was released in Guwahati, Assam by Union Minister for Electronics & Information Technology Ravi Shankar Prasad.
- President Ram Nath Kovind has Assam Witch Hunting (Prohibition, Prevention and Protection) Bill, 2015 passed by State Assembly in August 2015. This law aims to reign in rising incidents of witch hunting cases across the state.
- Numaligarh Refinery Ltd (NRL) in Assam became first oil public sector undertaking (PSU) in India to adopt an online legal compliance system by introducing 'Legatrix'.
- Assam Spring Festival organised at Manas National Park.
- Hima Das : The United Nations Children's Fund-India (UNICEF) on November 14, 2018 appointed Asian Games gold-medalist sprinter 18 years old girl of Assam, Hima Das as India's first ever Youth Ambassador.
  UNICEF India works along with the Central Government to ensure that children born in India get the best start in life, thrive and develop to his or her full potential.

1 Government of Assam

❍ **Governor**	**Shri Jagdish Mukhi**
❍ **Chief Minister**	**Shri Sarbananda Sonowal**
❍ **Speaker**	**Shri Hitendra Nath Goswami**
❍ **Deputy Speaker**	**Shri Kripanath Mallah**

Council of Ministers

Shri Sarbananda Sonowal	:	Home, Political, Personnel, GAD, SAD, Implementation of Assam Accord Administrative Reform & Training, Election, I & PR, Border Area Development, Sports & Youth Welfare, Revenue and DM and any other department not allotted to the other Ministers.
Dr. Himanta Biswa Sarma	:	Finance, Transformation & Development, Health & Family Welfare, PWD
Shri Atul Bora	:	Agriculture, Horticulture and Food Processing, Animal Husbandry and Veterinary, Town & Country Planning
Smt. Pramila Rani Brahma	:	Social Welfare, Soil Conservation
Shri Keshab Mahanta	:	Water Resources, Science & Technology, Information Technology, Cultural Affairs (Only Library & Archeology matters)
Shri Parimal Sukla Baidya	:	Fishery, Excise, Environment & Forest
Shri Ranjit Dutta	:	Handloom and Textile and Sericulture (including Khadi and Village Industry), Welfare of Minorities

Shri Chandra Mohan Patowary :	Commerce and Industry, Transport, Parliamentary Affairs, Act East Policy Affairs, Skill Entrepreneur & Employment
Shri Siddhartha Bhattacharya :	Education (Higher, Secondary Elementary), GDD, Law & Justice
Shri Sum Ronghang :	Hills Area Development, Mines & Minerals.
Shri Phani Bhusan Choudhury :	Food & Civil Supplies and Consumer Affairs, Pension & Public Grievance
Shri Chandan Brahma :	Tourism, Welfare of Plain Tribes and Backward Classes
Shri Rihan Daimary :	Public Health Engineering, Co-operation,

Ministers of State (Independent Charge)

Shri Naba Doley :	Panchayat and Rural Development (Independent), Cultural Affairs excluding Library & Archeology matters (Independent), Environment & Forest (assist Cabinet Minister as MoS)
Shri Pallab Lochan Das :	Labour and Employment (Independent), Tea Tribes Welfare (Independent), Education (assist Cabinet Minister as MoS)
Shri Bhabesh Kalita :	Irrigation (Independent), Revenue and DM (assist Hon'ble CM as MoS)
Shri Topon Kumar Gogoi :	Power (Independent) , PWD (assist Cabinet Minister as MoS)
Shri Pijush Hazarika :	Urban Development excluding T&CP (Independent), Health & FW (assist Cabinet Minister as MoS)

2 Assam at a Glance

The word Assam is derived from the Sanskrit word "ASOMA" meaning peerless. The natural beauty of Assam is one of the most enchanting in the country with majestic rivers, rich landscape, lofty green hills, evergreen forests, lushy grass plains, rarest flora and fauna, beautiful islands and virtually everything. Moreover, the humbleness, hospitality and simplicity of the people residing here add a grace to the beauty of this magical valley, making it unique in itself and not only this, each place of this mystical valley has something celestial and astonishing to offer. So, many people call it a 'Magical Land'.

Dispur is the capital city of Assam. Assam is surrounded by the states of Arunachal Pradesh in the east and north-east, Nagaland, Manipur, Mizoram, Tripura and Meghalaya in the south, and it has also common international boundary of 500 km with Bhutan and 200 km with Bangladesh. Assam is situated between 90° and 96° East Longitude and 24° and 28° North Latitude and has a total area of 78,438 sq km. about 2.39 percent of the country's total geographical area. Assam receives the highest amount of rainfall among other north east states.

The state is known for its tea, petroleum resources, muga silk and bio-diversity. It is also becoming an increasingly popular destination for wildlife tourism. The state is rich in water resources and has vast tracts of fertile land. Assam is also the third-largest producer of petroleum and natural gas in the country and has ample reserves of limestone. With its five national parks and 18 wildlife sanctuaries, the state is a biodiversity hotspot. Other potential areas of investment include power and energy, mineral-based industries, tourism and crude oil refining.

Assam is known to many as a nightmarish land of earthquakes. As Assam is situated in a zone inclined to earthquakes, so, the state, very often, experiences earthquake tremors. Among the most severe are those recorded in 1897, with the Shillong Plateau as the epicentre; in 1930, with Dhuburi as the epicentre; and in 1950, with Zayu (Rima) in Tibet at the Arunachal Pradesh border as the epicentre. The 1950 earthquake is considered one of the most disastrous in South Asia's history. It created heavy landslides that blocked the courses of many hill streams. The floods that followed the bursting of those earthquake-generated dams caused more loss of life and property than the earthquake itself.

Some Basic Facts About Assam		
• **Capital**	:	Dispur
• **State Assembly Seats**	:	126
• **Lok Sabha Seats**	:	14
• **Rajyasabha Seats**	:	7
• **State Emblem**	:	One Horned Indian Rhino.
• **State Animal**	:	One Horned Indian Rhino
• **State Bird**	:	The White winged wood duck
• **State Flower**	:	The Fox-tail orchid
• **State Tree**	:	The Hollong
• **Area**	:	78,438 sq. km. (approx.)
• **Population (2011)**	:	31,205,576
– **Male**	:	15,939,443
– **Female**	:	15,266,133
• **Density** (persons per sq. km .) (2011)	:	398
• **Sex Ratio** (2011) (*females per 1000 males*)	:	958
• **Decadal Growth Rate** (2001 -2011)	:	17.07%
• **Literacy Rate** (2011)		72.19%
• **Districts**	:	Barpeta, Bongaigaon, Chirang, Darrang, Dhemaji, Dhubri, Goalpara, Dibrugarh, Tinsukia, Golaghat, Jorhat, Lakhimpur, Morigaon, Sivasagar, Sonitpur, Kamrup , Nagaon, Nalbari, Kokrajhar, Cachar, Dima Hasao, Hailakandi, Karbi Anglong, Karimganj, Baksa, Udalguri, Kamrup (Metropolitan), Biswanath Charial, Hojai, Karbi Anglong, Charaidev ,South Salmora Mankachar and Majuli island (India's first island district)
• **Major Cities**	:	Guwahati, Rangia, Dibrugarh, Tezpur, Silchar, Jorhat, etc.
• **Seat of High Court**	:	Guwahati
• **Wildlife Sanctuaries**	:	18
• **Major Rivers**	:	Brahmaputra and Barak.
• **Major Languages**	:	Assamese, Bodo, Hindi, Bengali, etc.
• **Major Festivals**	:	Bihu, Durga Puja, Diwali, Holi, Eid, Christmas, etc.
• **Agriculture**	:	80% population in dependent on agriculture
• **Cash Crops**	:	Tea ,Jute, Cotton, Potato
• **Main Cereal Crop**	:	Rice
• **Forest Products**	:	Wood, Bamboo, Cane, Herbs and Ivory
• **Major Religions**	:	Hinduism, Buddhism, Jainism, Sikhism, Islam and Christianity.
• **Major Tribes**	:	Bodo Kachari, Karbi, Mishing, Sonowal, Kacharis, Tiwas, Dimasa, Garo, Deuris, Chutias, Varmans, Hajong, etc.
• **Assam Chief Minister**	:	Sarbananda Sonowal
• **Governor**	:	Jagdish Mukhi

3 Geography of Assam

Geographically Assam is situated in the North-eastern region of the Indian sub-continent. It is located between 24°10'N to 27°58'N Latitude and 89°49'E to 97°26'E Longitude. It covers an area of 78,52,359 Kilometers (approximate). Assam-the gateway of North East India is a land of blue hills, valley and rivers. The Capital of Assam is Dispur and the state emblem is one-hoed rhino. Assam is bounded by Manipur, Nagaland and Myanmar in the east and the rest by west Bengal in the north by Bhutan and Arunachal Pradesh and in the route by Mizoram, and Bangladesh and Meghalaya. The Physiography of Assam is one of the most enchanting in the country. It can be broadly classified into three well defined geographical regions.

1. The Brahamputra River Valley.
2. The Barak Valley.
3. The hilly regions comprising the North Cachar Hill (Now Dima Hasao) and the Karbi Anglong district which separate the two valleys.

Brahamputra River Valley

A major population of Assam resides in the vast Brahamputra valley in the north Amidst numerous mountains, stream and rivulets from the nearby hills, this extended valley offers a enchanting view and is a great attraction among tourists and travelers.

The mighty river enters the state after gorging through Arunachal Pradesh. It runs south-east and finally merges with the Gangas, to form a vast delta. Its entire course can be navigated from the Barak valley to the district of Dibrugarh. Based on the flow of Brahamputra River, the entire state of Assam can be divided into two parts upper and lower Assam. The major districts that come under upper Assam are Digboi, Duliajan, Tinsukia, Dibrugarh, Sibsagar, Jorhat and Golaghat. The district that fall under lower Assam include Dhermaji, Nalbari, Barpeta, Kokrajhar and Bongaigaon.

Barak Valley

The Southern zone or the Barak valley region of Assam is, in fact, an extension of the neighbouring country Bangladesh. The major districts of the region are Karimganj, Cachar and Hailakandi.

Karbi Anglong and North Cachar Hills

Karbi Anglong , in the central part of Assam, covers a total area of 10,434 square kilometer and is the largest district of the state. It is also home to some major tribes like the Bodos, Kukis, Dimasas, Tiwas Gados and Khasis to the south of the district lies the districts of North Cachar and Nagaland.

Climate

Assam is temperate region and experiences heavy rainfall and humidity. The location, situation and topography of Assam make its climate different from rest of India. The weather is dry in winter and hot and wet in summer. The Himalayan range protect Assam from cold wind from central Asia in winter but causes heavy rain as it obstruct the South-west wind from over running. In winter, the western/Mediterranean disturbances influence the climate of Assam to some extent by causing rainfall and fog. Sandstorms, fog and cyclones are some local factors which influences the climate of Assam.

Rain fall

The state of Assam records one of the highest rainfall in the world. The heavy monsoon rain normally begins from early June and it lasts up to September or the first part of October.

IMPORTANT RIVERS AND THEIR TRIBUTARIES

Rivers	Tributaries
1. Brahamputra	Subansiri, Puthimari, Pagladiya, Manas, Na-Dihing, Disang, Bornodi, Burhi-Dihing, Bhoroli, Dikhow, Dhansiri, Kapili, Jiyadhol, Ronganoi, Kakodonga, Dibru, Sampaboti, Buroi, Dudhoni, Krishnai, Dikong, Bhagdoi, etc.
2. Barak	Jatinga, Sonai, Bogapani, Jiri, Singra, Jadukata, Longai etc.
3. Subansiri	Sarikoria, Kumotiya, Jiyadhol.
4. Na-Dihing	Dirak
5. Dibru	Dangari, Dumduma.
6. Buri-Dihing	Tipling, Tingrai, Namsang, Sancha.
7. Kakodonga	Dholi
8. Dhansiri	Daiyang, Nambar, Koliyoni.
9. Manas	Ai
10. Kapili	Borapani, Jamuna, Kiling.

(Lakes of Assam)

Chandubi

This is a natural lagoon situated at a distance of 64 km from Guwahati Fishing and boating facilities are available here.

Tamranga

It is located in Bongaiguon. The lake is considered as ornithologist's paradise as a large number of migratory birds here during winter.

Padum Pukhuri

Padum Pakhuri, one of the most famous landmarks of Tazpur is a famous lake with an island which converted into park having musical fountains.

Urpad Beel

Urpad Beel is situated at Agia in Goalpara district. It is one of the biggest lake of lower Assam. Besides its natural beauty, the lake is rich in natural resources. Every year a number of migratory birds visit the lake during October to March.

Deepor Beel

A wetland lying on south - Northern part of Guwahati, which has been listed on Ramsar list of wetland. It support some endangered species of birds like Spotbilled Pelican, Lessez Adjutant Stork, Baer's Pochard, Palas Sea Eagle, Greater Adjutant Strok.

Son Beel

It is the largest fresh water tectonic lake in Assam lies in the Southern part of the state. It is situated in the Northern part of Karimganj district and also covers some portion of the district Hailakandi. The Singla river, which flows from Mizoram serves the in let of the Beel, while the Kachua river originating from the Northern part of the Beel the main outlet.

Halflong

It is one of the natural Lakes on the hilly station of Assam. Boating and hot water spring are the major tourist attractions on this lake.

Minerals of Assam

Assam is an important state of India with varieties of minerals. The largest industries in Assam are Oil, Tea and Hydrocarbon. Geographically Assam lies in an oil Rich belt. A small quantity of Iron is also available in Western part of Assam.

In 1899 the Assam oil company was formed as several oil seepages were observed in the districts of upper Assam. It is estimated that Assam and surrounding region possess around 150 million tonnes of petroleum reserves. Natural gas is another valuable source of power and various other chemical by-products. In Assam, almost all the petroleum producing areas of the Brahmaputra Valley contains 'associated natural gas'.

4 History of Assam

Assam a name is derived from the Sanskrit word "ASOMA" meaning "Peerless" or 'unparallel' is located south of eastern Himalayas and is home of the Sun of Lord Brahma which perhaps accounts for the Brahmaputra River being the only male river in India.

Its ancient history has been from literature and historical stories like Mahabharata and during the epic period of India history Assam was named "Pragiyotishpura" meaning place of eastern astronomy. It was referred to as the kamarupa kingdom from the 4th –12th century and its medieval history is dominated by the Ahoms a Tai group that migrated from what is now Yunnan in China and ruled Assam for nearly 600 years (1228-1826) and the Tibeto-Burmese koch whose kingdom split in two, one group allying will the Moguls and the other will the Ahoms. Ahoms-Mogol conflict finally ended in 1682 will a mogul defeat.

Assam repelled numerous invasions, mostly led by Muslim rulers but with the waning of Ahom power the Burmese overran the entire territory in the early 19th century. It was then ceded to the British in 1826 the first and only western power to ever rule Assam in 1874 a separate province of Assam was created with shillong as its capital. It become a state of the Union of India when India attained independence in 1947 then, after Assam was divided in 1972, shillong was made capital of the new state of Meghalaya and Dispur located near the city of Guwahati became Assam's new capital.

The Varmana Dynasty : The real political history of ancient Assam begins with the foundation of the Varmana line of kings. The inscription of Bhaskaravarman, the greatest king of this dynasty as well as of ancient Assam, Banabhatta's Harshacharita and the accounts of the Chinese pilgrim Hiuem-Tsang furnish considerable materials relating to the history of the Varmanas. It is learnt from epigraphical sources that Pushyavarman, born in the lineage of Naraka - Bhagaduta was the founder of the Varmana of Bhauma line of kings. When and how Pushyavarman came to power is not known. He probably taking advantage of the political instability of the time, made himself king and to justify his claim, traced his descent from Naraka-Bhagadutta. According to B.M. Barua."

Pushyavarman was the first Indo-Aryan ruler set up by Samudragupta over the two territories of Kamarupa and Davaka unified into a single kingdo." But this view is not tenable because Pushyavarman assumed the important title of Maharajadhiraja which indicates his independent status. Pushyavarman was probably a contemporary of Samudragupta. In the Allahabad pillar inscription of this Gupta emperor, the name of Kamrupa occurs as a frontier kingdom Samalata, Dvaka, Nepal and Kartipur, whose kings owed allegiance to Samudragupta on their own accord. The unnamed king of Kamarupa of this inscription is usually identified with Pushyavarman. If we count the date of Pushyavarman on the basis of the Badaganga epigraph of Bhutivarman, (dated 234 Gupta era which corresponds to 553-54 A.D.) who was the eighth king of the dynasty and allow its king an average reigning period of 25 years, Pushyavarman's reign would fall between c.355-80 A.D. he would thus be a contemporary of Samudragupta (C.320-80 A.D.). It was perhaps in honour of his overlord that he name his son as Samudravarman and his daughter-in-law as Dattadevi in imitation of the names of the Gupta emperor Samudragupta and his queen Dattadevi.

During the reign of kalyanavarman, the son of Balavarman, the Davaka or the Kapili valley (comprising possibly the present district of Nagoan, Karbi Anglong and North Cachar area) was absorbed into the empire Kamarupa. To signalise this victory, he sent a diplomatic mission to china in 428 A.D. Mahendravarman, grandson of Kalyanvarman expanded his empire to s**outh-east** Bengal upto the sea by shaking off the last vestiges of the Gupta influence in Kmarupa. He was the first king of Assam to perform Aswamedha and he did it on two occasions. Mahendra-varman's grandson Bhutiavarman was a powerful king. He conquered Pundravardhana (North Bengal) Sometime between 545-50 A.D. and donated lands to more than 200 Brahmanas in the Chandrapuri visaya located within the Pundravardhana bhukti. He might have also extended his sway in the south and the west and brought the outlying regions of Samatata, Sylhet, Tripura and other regions under his control. He has also performed one Aswamedha sacrifice. The glory of Kamarupa suffered a temporary set back during the reign of Bhaskaravar man's father Susthitavarman, who suffered a defeat at the hands of the Later Gupta monarch Mahasenagupta and as a result of this defeat lost the possession of Pundravardhana. Bhaskaravarman (c.600-650 A.D.).

During the reign of Bhaskaravarman that the great Chinese pilgrim Houen Tsang Kamrupa in 643 A.D. and stayed in his capital for nearly two months. The pilgrim speaks highly about the noble qualities of Bhaskara and his prowess. In the religious assemblies held at Prayag and Kanauj by harsha, Bhaskara was shown special honour in the presence of all the kings assembled there. After the death of Harsha in 648 A.D., Bhaskara became the supreme lord of Eastern India extending his sway as far as Nalanda. He had also brought under his control Sylhet and Tripura including south-east Bengal. This is testified by Hiuen Tsang who refers to Bhaskara as "King of eastern India" and stated that the rules of Kamarupa had the sea-route to China under their protection. Inscriptions bear testimony to the many-sided qualities and achievements of centre of learning attracting students from outside. With the expansion of the political sway of the Varmana line of kings large portion of Eastern India came under the cultural ideas of Kamarupa. This influence ever spread to the islands in the pacific and some of the architectural remains in Combodia, Annam and other places are possibly to be attributed to the influence of the rulers of Kamarupa.

Salasthmbha Dynasty

The Salasthambha dynasty was the next in the line which began with the reign of a chieftain called Salasthambha. Among all the kings of the Salasthambha dynasty, it was Shri Harshadeva (728-750 AD) who acquitted himself as a good king. After the last king of this dynasty, Tyaga Singha (970-990), it was Brahmapala (990-1010 AD), who opened the door to a new dynasty - the Pala dynasty. Jayapala (1120-1138 AD) was the last ruler of this (Pala) dynasty.

Pala Dynasty

Tyagasigha possible died childless but the danger of rebellion centering round his heirless death was tactfully avoided by the officers by choosing Brahmapala to the throne he established a new dynasty named Pala dynasty. His son Ratanapala ruled over this kingdom for about 30 years and was followed by Indrapala as his successor. They ruled over Kamarupa for about 200 years. Prithu (1200 - 1228 AD), a powerful king came to power immediately after the fall of Pala dynasty, successfully repeated the first Muslim invasion of Kamarupa, but was thrown out from power after the second Muslim invasion in 1228 AD.

Sutiya Kingdom

This kingdom was established on the north bank of the river Brahamputra in north-eastern Assam and parts of Arunachal Pradesh by Birpal. The Sutiyas were a Tibeto- Burmese race who secured power in Assam at the same time as the Khen kings and Barobhuyan chieftains (to the west), during the decline of kamarupa kingdom. The claimed descent from remnants of the former Mlechha kings of Assam. He was succeeded by ten kings of whom the eighth king Dhirnarayan or Dharmadhwajpal, in his old age, handed over his kingdom to his son-in-law Nitai or Nityapal. Later on Nityapal's incompetent rule gave a wonderful chance to the Ahom king Suhungmung or Dihingia Raja, who annexed it to the Ahom kingdom.

Ahom Rule

The Ahoms belonged to the Shan Tai Meng Mao race which originated in parts of southern china and south-east Asia. Adopting the Hindu religion they formed kingdom in regions of Kamarupa (in Assam) in the early thirteenth century. They also gave their name to the region, Ahom being the ancient version of the Anglicised Assam.

The largest of these kingdoms was formed by Sukhapa, a Shan prince who was captured part of Assam after descending from the Patkai mountains. He ruled from his capital at Charaideo. The base for 600 years of Ahom rule was set up by Sukafa. Sukafa died in 1268 AD. His son Suseupha (1268-1281) succeeded and extended the boundaries of the kingdom from the area adjoining Dikhow river at Namdang river. In 1397 Sudangpha (1397-1407) was established. His accession marks the first stage in the growth of Brahmanical influence amongst the Ahoms. A war between Ahoms and Tipams took place during his reign but was later on peacefully concluded.

It was Suhumgmung's reign (1497 -1539) which is counted as one of the most memorable in 600 year of Ahom rule. He was popularly known as Dihingia Raja, because he shifted the Ahom capital to Bokota near Dihing river. He annexed the Chutia and the Kachari territories to the Ahom domains. He created a third class of Ministers, Borgohain, Buragohain and Borpatra Gohain. The first ever census took place during his reign. The economic scenario of the State was also comprehensively surveyed. During his reign, the Mughala invaded thrice but they could not get victory. This invasion taught Ahoms the use of gunpower, which was a deviation from the traditional system of warfare which comprised of bows, arrows and swords.

The Mughal invasion had another positive effect, the Mughals who were taken as prisoner of war were settled in different areas of Assam. Letter on, they came to be popularly known as "Morias". Srimanta Sankardev got full impetus to preach his Vaishnava Dharma during the rule of Swarganarayan. In 1539 AD he died at the hands of a Kachari servant due to a conspiracy hatched by his-son Suklengmung (1539-1552), who after becoming king, shifted the capital to Gargoan from Bokota which is why he is called 'Gargainya Raja.

Susengpha, a descendant of Suklengmung, ascended the throne in 1603. He took on the name of Pratap Singha. During his period war between Ahoms and Mughals reached its peak and Pratap Singha acquitted himself with full honours and was able to extend the boundaries of the state,. He created a new post of Brarphukan to look after the administration of the areas beyond Kaliabor. The three classes of ministers Buragohain, Borgohain and Borpatra Gohain had their well defined areas to rule and those part of the kingdom which did not fall under their jurisdiction were brought under the control of Barbaruah, a new post created during the rule of Pratap Singha. Momai Tamuli Barbaruah was the first official to hold this post. Pratap Singha tried his best to upgrade the life of citizens. He also introduced Pyke (common rayat) system. Under this system, people were divided into groups of 1000, 100 and 20, and over groups- officials Hazarika, Sakia and Bora were elected. Creation of other post like Rohiyal Barua, Jagiyal Gohain, Kajalimukhiya Gohain is also credited to him. For his organizational capability, political acumen and his great wisdom, he is also known as Buddhi Swarganarayan.

Supungmung or Chakradhvaj Singha (1663-1669) prepared himself for another fight against the Mughals. He enlisted the help of Lachit Barphukan, who was the son of Momai Tamuli Barbaruah. In August 1667, under the excellent leadership of Lachit Barphukan, the Ahoms were able to get back Guwahati and Pandu. Hearing the news of this defeat Aurangzeb sent a huge force with Ramsingh to attack the Ahom kingdom once again. A fierce battle took place between the Ahoms and the Mughals in 1671 at Saraighat. As expected, the Mughals suffered and ignominious defeat. Consequently in the west the Manas river became the demarcation line between the Ahom and Mughal territories and remained so until the British occupation to 1826 AD.

Supatpha govern from Borkola, establishing the rule of the Tung khungia Clan. He retakes Guwahati from the Mughuls and proves to be a good administrator. He built 'Umananda Devaloi' at Guwahati. He also built the 'Dhodar Ali', a road near Golaghat. Gadadhar Singha's eldest son Lai succeeded him. He took on the Hindu name of Rudra Singha (1696 - 1714) and the Ahom name Sukrumpha. In the honour of the memory of his mother Joymoti, he dug the Joysagar tank. Other architectural monuments and structures accredited to him are Kareng Ghar, stone bridge built over the Namdang river, Kharikatia Ali, Metaka Ali. Rudra Singha gave royal patronage to 'Bihu'. He also created Khels or positions like Khaund, Kotoki, Bairagi, Dolai, Kakoti.

In (1714-1744) Sutanpha, son of Rudra Singha took on the Hindu name of Siva Singha. He became a Shakti worshiper, as he was initiated in the tenets of the Shakti cult by Krishnaram Bhattacharya, who was later on installed as head priest of Kamakhya temple which is situated on the peak of the Nilachal Hills. Siva Singha was. A weak person who strongly believe on astrologers which explains the fact that when an astrologer told him that he was in danger of being dethroned, he throned his Queen Phuleswari, who assumed the name Pramateswari (one of the names of Durga), as Bor Raj, or chief king, thus engineering the beginning of the end of the Ahom Dynasty. Phuleswari was an orthodox Shakti worshiper who persecuted the Moamoria Mahanta by forcibly making them to take Prasad of Durga worship and anointing their foreheads with sacrificial blood. This resulted in the famous Moamoria rebellion. After Phuleswari died in 1731, Siva Singha married her sister Drupadi or Deopadi and made her the next Bor Raja with the name Ambika. She was the one who constructed the Shiva Dol (temple) at Sibsagar, which is the biggest Shiva temple in Assam. It was during her reign that 'Dhai Ali' was constructed at Sibsagar. Gauri Sagar tank and Sibsagar tank were dug at the instruction of 'Bor Raja' Phuleswari and Ambika respectively.

Colonial Assam

British Annexation of Assam :

After the Burmese occupied Assam, the British began their campaign against the Burmese. In 1824, lower Assam (originally Koch Hajo) was formally annexed. The following year the British defeated the 'Burmese in upper Assam leading to the Treaty of Yandaboo. In this war against the Burmese the Ahoms did not help the British. In March 1828, lower Assam was formally annexed. In the same year, the Kachari Kingdom was annexed under the Doctrine of Lapse after the kind Govinda Chandra was killed. In 1832, the Khasi King surrendered and the British increased their influence over the Jaintia rular. In 1833, upper Assam was handed over to an erstwhile ruler of the Ahom kingdom. Purandhar Singha, as a protectorate of the British, but in 1838 the region was formally annexed into the British empire. With the annexation of the Maran/Matak territory in the east in 1839, the annexation of Assam was complete.

Bengal Presidency (1826-1873) :

Assam was included a part of the Bengal Presidency, The annexation of upper Assam is attributed to the successful manufacture of tea in 1837, and the beginning of Assam tea Company in 1839. Under the Wasteland Rules of 1838, it became nearly impossible for natives to start plantations. After liberalizations of the rules in 1854, there was a land rush, The Chinese staff that was imported earlier for the cultivation of tea, left Assam in 1843, when tea plantations came to be tended by local labour solely, mainly by Kachari group. From1859 central Indian labour was imported for the tea plantations. This labour based on an unbreakable contract, led to a virtual slavery of this labour group. The conditions in which they were transported to Assam were so horrific that about 10% never survived the journey. The colonial government already had monopoly over the opium trade.

There were immediate protest and revolts against the British occupation. In 1828, two year after the Treaty of Yandaboo, Gomdhar Konwar rose in revolt against the British. In 1830 Dhananjoy Burhagohain, Piyali Phukan and Jiuram Medhi rose in revolt, but they were sentenced to death. In the Indian rebellion of 1857, the people of Assam offered resistance in the form of non-cooperation, and Maniram Dewan and Piyali Baruah were executed for their roles. In 1861 peasants of Nagaon gathered at Phularguri for peoples assembly to protest against taxes on betel-nut and Paan. Lt. Singer, a British officer got into a fracas with the peasants and was killed, after which the protests were violently suppressed.

Chief Commissioner's Province (1874 - 1905)

In 1874, the Assam region was separated from Bengal Presidency, Sylhet was added to it and its status was upgraded to a Chief Commissioner's Province. The capital replaced by Bengali as the official language in 1837, was rein started alongside Bengali. In 1889, oil was discovered at Digboi giving rise to an oil industry. In the period Nagaon witnessed starvation deaths, and there was a decrease in the indigenous population on, Which was more than adequately compensated by the immigrant labour. Colonialism was well lodged and the tea, oil and coal-mining industries were putting increasing pressure on the agricultural sector. The peasants, burdened under the opium monopoly and the usury by money lenders, rose again in revolt. Numerous 'raiz mels' decided against paying the taxes. The protests culminated in a bayonet charge against the protesters at Patharughat in 1894. At least 15 were left dead and in the violent repression that followed, the villagers were tortured and their properties were destroyed. In 1903 Assam Association was formed with Manik Chandra Baruah as the first secretary.

Eastern Bengal and Assam Under Lt. Governor (1906-1912)

Bangal was partitioned and East Bengal was added to the Chief Commissioner's Province. The new region, now ruled by Lt. Governor, had its capital at Dhaka. This province had a 15-member legislative council in which Assam had two seats. The members for these seats were recommended by rotating groups of public bodies.

The Partition of Bengal was strongly protested in Bengal, and the people of Assam were not happy either. The partition was finally annulled by the royal decree in 1911. The Swadeshi movement (1905 - 1908) from this period, went largely unfelt in Assam, though it stirred some, most notably Ambikagiri Raychoudhury.

Beginning 1905 peasants from East Bengal began settling down in the riverine tracts (char) of the Brahmaputra valley encouraged by the colonial government to increase agricultural production, Between 1905 and 1921, the immigrant population from East Bengal increased four times. Post colonial immigration continued giving rise to the Assam agitation of 1979.

Assam Legislative council (1912 - 1920)

The administrative unit was reverted to a Chief Commissioner's Province (Assam plus) Commissioner and 13 nominated members formed the bulk. The other members were elected by local public bodies like municipalities, local boards. Landholders, tea planters and Muslims.

As Assam got stuck into the Non-Cooperation Movement, the Assam Association slowly transformed itself into the Assam Pradesh Congress Committee (with 5 seats in AICC) in 1920 - 1921.

Dyarchy (1921 - 1937)

Under the Government of India Act 1919 the Assam Legislative Council membership was increased to 53, of which 33 were elected by special constituencies. The power of the Council were increased too, but in effect, the official group, consisting of the Europeans, the nominated members etc, had the most influence.

Assam Legislative Assembly (1937 - 1947)

Under the Government of India act 1935, the Council was expanded into an Assembly of 108 members, with even more powers. The period saw the sudden rise of Gopinath Bordoloi and Muhammed Saadulah and their tussle for power and influence.

The first Governor of Independent Assam was Sir Akbar Haidari and Chief Minister was Gopinath Bordoli was saw the foundations laid of Gauhati University (1948). Gauhati High Court (1948), Guwahati Station of All India Radio.

Milestones in Assamese History
☞ Assam first appeared on the history map, as Pragiyotisa, long before the Christian era began.
☞ Assam came to be known as Kamrup, from the ancient to the medieval period.
☞ Naraka became this first known ruler of Assam.
☞ Bhagadatta, king of Assam, Participated in the Mahabharata war, as a hero.
☞ Barman Dynasty ruled over Assam from 7th century AD.
☞ Salastambha Dynasty ruled over Assam from 7th century to 10th century AD.
☞ Pala Dynasty ruled over Assam from 10th century to 13th century AD.
☞ Muslims invaded Assam in 1228 AD.
☞ Ahoms entered Assam from Burma in 1228 AD and created a new Chapter in Assamese history, ruled till the 19th century.
☞ Assam was annexed to British India in 1826.
☞ Assam became part of Independent India in 1947.

Assam Accord

In the years from 1979 to 1985 witnessed major political instability in the state collapse of state governments imposition of President's rule, sustained often violent, agitation, frequent general strikes, civil disobedience campaigns which paralyzed all normal life for prolonged periods and unprecedented ethnic violence . The 1983 violence had a traumatic effect on both sides, which once again resumed negotiations in earnest. Finally the Rajiv government was able to sign an accord with the leaders of the movement on 15 August 1985.

Some of the major clauses of the historic Accord an as follows : –

Clause 1 : For purpose of detection and deletion of foreigners, 01.01.1996 shall be the base data and year.

Clause 2 : All persons who came to Assam prior to 01.01.1966 including those amongst them whose name appeared on the electoral rolls used in 1967 elections shall be regularised.

Clause 3 : Foreigners who came to Assam after 01.01.1966 (inclusive) and upto 24th March 1971 shall be detected in accordance with the provisions of the Foreigners Act. 1946 and the Foreigners order 1939.

Clause 4 : Name of foreigners, so detected will be deleted from the electoral rolls in force. Such persons will be required to register themselves before the Registration Officers of the respective district in accordance with the provisions of the Registration of Foreigners Act, 1939 and the Registration of Foreigners Act, 1939.

Clause 5 : For this purpose, Government of India will undertake suitable strengthening of the government machinery.

Clause 6 : On the expiry of period of 10 years following the date of detection, the names of all such persons which have been deleted from the electoral rolls shall be restored.

Clause 7 : All persons who were expelled earlier, but have since reentered illegally into Assam shall be expelled.

Clause 8 : Foreigners who came to Assam on or after March 25, 1971 shall continue to be detected, deleted and practical steps shall be taken to expel such foreigners.

Clause 9 : The Government will give due consideration to certain difficulties expressed by the AASU/AAGSP regarding the implementation of the Illegal Migrants (Determination by Tribunals) Act, 1983.

5 Administration

The Assam Legislative Assembly is the Unicameral Legislative of the India State of Assam. It is housed in Dispur, the capital of Assam. The Legislative Comprises 126 members of Legislative Assembly directly elected from single seat constituencies. Its term is five year. The state is represented 7 member in the Rajya Sabha and 14 members of the Lok Sabha.The Governor is the constitutional head of the state, who is appointed by the central Government for a certain period.

Assam is divided into 35 district including Majuli (the first river island district of India). The Districts of Assam are grouped together in five regional divisions, headed by a commissioner. A superintendent of police, an officer belonging to Indian Police service is entrusted with the responsibility of maintaining law and order and related Issues. The police administration in Guwahati city is headed by the Commissioner of Police.

Note

The Assam Government has granted district status to Majuli a 400 sq. kilometer island in the Brahmaputra River. With this it becomes India's first Island district. With this erosion-troubled Majuli Island will become the 35th district of Assam. Earlier it was sub division of Jorhat district.

Administrative Units

Districts	:	35
Sub - Division	:	58
Towns	:	214
Blocks	:	219
Villages	:	26,395
Number of Gaon Panchayats	:	2,489

Districts and Their Headquarters

Code	District	Headquarter
BA	Barpeta	Barpeta
BO	Bongaigaon	Bongaigaon
CA	Cachar	Silchar

DA	Darrang	Mangaldai
DM	Dhemaji	Dhemaji
DB	Dhubri	Dhubri
DI	Dibrugarh	Dibrugar
GP	Goalpara	Goalpara
GG	Golaghat	Golaghat
HA	Hailakandi	Hailakhandi
JO	Jorhat	Jorhat
KA	Karbi Anglong	Diphu
KR	Karimganj	Karimganj
KK	Kokrajhar	Kokrajhar
LA	Lakhimpur	North Lakhimpur
MA	Morigaon	Morigaon
NG	Nogaon	Nagaon
NL	Nalbari	Nalbari
NC	Dima Hasoa	Haflong
SI	Sivasagar	Sivasagar
SO	Sonitpur	Tezpur
TI	Tinsukia	Tinsukia
	Kamrup	Amingaon
	Kamrup Metropolitan	Guwahati
	Baksa	Mushalpur
	Udalguri	Udalguri
	Chirang	Kajalgaon
	West Karbi Anglong	Hamren
	Biswanath	Biswanath Chariali
	Hojai	Hojai
	Charaideo	Sonari
	South Salmara-Mankachar	Hatsingimari
	East Kamrup	Dispur

	South Kamrup	Plasbari
	Majuli	Garmur

Autonomous Council

There are Nine autonomous council in the state :

1. North Cachar Hills Council
2. Karbi Anglong Council
3. Rabha Council
4. Tiwa Council
5. Mishing Council
6. Deori Council
7. Sonowal Kachari
8. Thengal Kachari
9. Bodolamel Territorial Council

Lok Sabha Constituencies of Assam

1. Autonomous district (ST)	2. Barpeta
3. Dhubri	4. Dibrugarh
5. Guwahati	6. Jorhat
7. Kaliabar	8. Karimganj
9. Kokrajhar	10. Lakhimpur
11. Mangoldol	12. Nagaon
13. Silchar	14. Tezpur

Judiciary

The Assam Judiciary is divide into the Assam High Court that is situated in the city of Guwahati and the district courts of the state. The Judiciary works effectively meeting out laws and maintaining order in the state.

The Assam High Court was established on April 5, 1948. The High Court has the strength of 23 judges and additional judges and its presided over by the honourable Chief Justice of Assam. The High Court has the powers of legislation over the other subsidiary courts and tribunals. It can issue territorial laws and orders over the encompassing area of its control.

The Chief Justice of the High Court is an important component of the judiciary system. The first Chief Justice of the Guwahati High Court was Sir R.F Lodge. The position is sacred to the judicial system and is highly respected.

Governors of Assam

Before Independence

Name	Tenure
Sir Henry Joseph Tuynam	24 Feb. 1938 - 04 Oct. 1939
Sir Robert Neil Reid	05 Oct. 1939 - 03 May 1942
Andrew Gourlay Clow	04 May 1942
Rederik Chalmers Bourne	04 April 1946
Sir Henry Foley Knight	04 Sept. 1946 - 23 Dec. 1946
Andrew Gourlay Clow	24 Dec. 1946 - 03 May 1947

During And After Independence

Name	Tenure
Sir Akbar Hydari	04 May, 1947 - 28 Dec. 1948
Ronald Francis	30 Dec. 1948 - 15 Feb. 1949
Sri Prakash	16 Feb. 1949 - 26 May 1950
Jairam Das Daulatram	27 May 1950 - 14 May 1956
Saiyid Fazal Ali	15 May 1956 - 22 Aug. 1959
Chandreswar Prasad Sinha	23 Aug. 1959 - 13 Oct. 1959
S M Shrinagesh	14 Oct. 1959 - 12 Nov. 1960
Vishnu Sahay	12 Nov. 1960 - 12 Jan. 1961
S M Shrinagesh	12 Jan. 1961 - 7 Sept. 1962
Vishnu Sahay	07 Sept. 1962 - 16 April 1968
B k Nehru	17 April 1968 - 07 Dec. 1970
Justice P. K. Swami	08 Dec. 1970 - 04 Jan. 1971
B K Nehru	05 Jan. 1971 - 18n Sept. 1973
Lalan Prasad Singh	19 Sept. 1973 - 10 Aug. 1981
Praksh Mehrotra	10 Aug. 1981 - 27 March 1984
T. S. Mishra	28 March. 1984 -15 April 1984
B. N. Singh	15 April 1984 - 10 May 1989
Harideo Joshi	10 May 1989 - 21 July 1989
Justice Anisetti Roghuvir	21 July 1989 - 02 May 1990
Devi Das Thakur	02 May 1990 - 17 March 1991
Lok Nath Mishra	17 March 1991 - 01 Sept. 1997
S. K. Sinha	01 Sept. 1997 - 21 April 2003
Arvind Dave	21 April 2003 - 05 June 2003

Ajai Singh	05 June 2003 - 04 July 2008
Charan Mathur	04 July 2008 - 17 July 2009
Syeb Sibte Rizvi	18 July 2009 - 27 Nov. 2009
Janaki Ballav Patnaik	28 Nov. 2009 - 11 Dec. 2014
Padmana Bha Balakrishna Acharya	12 Dec. 2014 - 17 Aug. 2016
Jagdish Mukhi	10 Oct. 2017 - Incumbent

Chief Ministers of Assam

Before Independence	
Name	**Tenure**
Syed Muhammad Sadulla	April 01, 1937 - Sept. 19, 1938
Gopinath Bordoloi	Sept 19, 1938 - Nov. 17, 1939
Syed Muhammad Sadulla	Nov. 17, 1939 - Dec. 24, 1941
Syed Muhammad Sadulla	Aug.25, 1942 - Feb. 11, 1946

During And After Independence	
Name	**Tenure**
Gopinath Bordoloi	Feb. 11, 1946 - Aug. 06, 1950
Bishnu Ram Medhi	Aug. 09, 1950 - Dec. 27, 1957
Bimala Prasad Chaliha	Dec. 28, 1957 - Nov. 06, 1970
Mahendra Mohan Choudhury	Nov. 11, 1970 - Jan 30, 1972
Sarat Chandra Sinha	Jan. 31, 1972 - March, 12, 1978
Golap Borbora	Mar. 12, 1978 - Sept. 09, 1979
Jogendra Nath Hazarika	Sept. 09, 1979 - Dec. 11, 1979
Sayeda Anowara Taimur	Dec. 12, 1980 - June 30, 1981
Keshab Chandra Gogoi	Jan. 13, 1982 - March.19, 1982
Hiteswar Saikia	Feb. 27, 1983 - Dec 23, 1985
Prafulla Kumar Mahanta	Dec. 24, 1985 - Nov. 27, 1990
Hiteswar Saikia	June 30, 1991 - April 22, 1996
Dr. Bhumindra Barman (Acting)	April 22, 1996 - May 14, 1996
Prafulla Kumar Mhanata	May 15, 1996 - May 17, 2001
Tarun Gogoi	May 18, 2001 - 24 May 2016
Sarbananda Sonowal	24 May 2016 - Incumbent

6 Population (Census-2011)

According to the Census of India, 2011 the population of Assam stands at 31,205,576 of which 15,939,443 are males and 15,266,133 females. The decadal growth of the State's population works out to 17.07% during the decade 2001-2011 as against 17.64% for the country as a whole. The state is spread over an area of about 78,438 sq. km. Making it the 16th largest state in the country in terms of area. The density of the population of Assam has gone upto 398 in 2011 which was 340 in 2001 Census. In 2011 Census the density of population of India was 382 as against State's density 398. Literacy rate in Assam has seen upward trend and is 72.19% as per 2011 population census. Of that, male literacy stands at 77.85% while female literacy is at 66.27%. In 2001, literacy rate in Assam stood at 63.25% of which male and female were 71.28% and 54.61% literate respectively.

Rural and Urban (Population) : As per population census, 2011, the rural population of the state is 85.90% of the total population. This percentage was much higher than that for All-India (69%). The proportion of rural population in the state decreased from 87% in 2001 to 85.90% in 2011. As per the population census, 2011 around 14.10% of the state population was living in urban areas. The proportion of urban population in the state increased from 12.9% in 2001 to 14.10% in 2011. The total figure of population living in urban areas is 4,398,542 of which 2,260,454 are males and while remaining 2,138,088 are females.

Assam Literacy Rate : The growth of Literacy in Assam has been upward trend and is 72.19% as per 2011 population census, of the total male literacy stands at 77.85% while females literacy is at 66.27%. In 2001 literacy rate in Assam stood at 63.25% of which male and female were 71.28% and 54.61% respectively. The literacy rates for rural and urban area found at 69.34% and 88.47% respectively. In actual numbers, total literacy in Assam stand at 19,507,07.

Density of Assam : Total area of Assam is 78,438 sq. km. Density of Assam is 398 per. sq. km. which was 340 in 2001 census. The corresponding all India figure was 382 as per census, 2011.

Assam Sex Ratio : Sex ratio in Assam is 958 *i.e.*, for each 1000 males, which is below national average of 940 as per census 2011. In 2001, the sex ratio of females was 935 per 1000 males in Assam.

ASSAM: CENSUS 2011

Description	2011	2001
Population	31,205,576	26,655,528
Male	15,939,443	13,777,037
Female	15,266,133	12,878,491
Population Growth	17.07%	18.85%
Sex Ratio	958	935
Child Sex Ratio	962	965
Density/km^2	398	340
Area (km^2)	78,438	78,438
Total Child Population (0-6 age)	4,638,130	4,498,075
Male population (0-6 age)	2,363,485	2,289,116
Female population (0-6 age)	2,274,645	2,208,959
Average Literacy	72.19 %	63.25%
Male Literacy	77.85 %	71.3%
Female Literacy	66.27 %	54.61%
Total Literates	19,177,977	14,015,354
Male Literates	10,568,639	8,188,697
Female Literates	8,609,338	5,826,657

Rural – Urban disparities as per 2011 Census

Population	Assam	Rural	Urban
Total Population	31,205,576	26,807,034	4,398,542
Male Population	15,939,443	13,678,989	2,260,454
Female Population	15,266,133	13,128,045	2,138,088
Population Growth	17.07%	15.47 %	27.89%
Sex Ratio	958	960	946
Child Population (0-6 age)	4,638,130	4,187,323	450,807
Average Literacy	72.19 %	69.34 %	88.47 %
Male Literacy	77.85 %	75.40 %	91.81 %
Female Literacy	66.27 %	60.05 %	79.85 %

Assam: Population Density as per Census 2011

The population density of the Assam state is 497 per sq km as per 2011 Census. It is comparatively higher than national average, which is 382 persons per sq km. As per 2001 census, the population density of Assam was 340 per persons per square km.

Rank	Name of the district	Population Density (Persons per sq. km.)
1	Kamrup Metropolitan	1999
2	Dhubri	1171
3	Nalbari	764
4	Nagaon	711
5	Karimganj	679
6	Barpeta	633
7	Morigaon	617
8	Goalpara	553
9	Darrang	502
10	Udalguri	497
10	Hailakandi	497
11	Baksa	473
12	Cachar	459
13	Lakhimpur	458

Rank	Name of the district	Population Density (Persons per sq. km.)
14	Kamrup	436
15	Sivasagar	431
16	Bongaigaon	428
17	Dibrugarh	392
18	Jorhat	383
19	Sonitpur	364
20	Tinsukia	350
21	Golaghat	305
22	Kokrajhar	280
23	Chirang	244
24	Dhemaji	212
25	Karbi Anglong	92
26	Dima Hasao	44

LIST OF DISTRICTWISE POPULATION, LITERACY & SEX RATIO IN ASSAM

List of districts of Assam with Population, Literacy rate, Sex Ratio etc. As per the Census 2011, Assam is divided into 27 districts (zilla) which act as the administrative divisions. Nagaon is the largest district of Assam by population, while the least populated district of Assam is Dima Hasao.

Below is the complete list of districts (zilla) of Assam sorted by population.

Sl.No.	District	Population	Literacy	Sex Ratio
1.	Nagaon	2,823,768	72.37%	962
2.	Dhubri	1,949,258	58.34%	953
3.	Sonitpur	1,924,110	67.34%	956
4.	Cachar	1,736,617	79.34%	959
5.	Barpeta	1,693,622	63.81%	953
6.	Kamrup	1,517,542	75.55%	949
7.	Tinsukia	1,327,929	69.66%	952
8.	Dibrugarh	1,326,335	76.05%	961

Sl.No.	District	Population	Literacy	Sex Ratio
9.	Kamrup Metropolitan	1,253,938	88.71%	936
10.	Karimganj	1,228,686	78.22%	963
11.	Sivasagar	1,151,050	80.41%	954
12.	Jorhat	1,092,256	82.15%	962
13.	Golaghat	1,066,888	77.43%	964
14.	Lakhimpur	1,042,137	77.2%	968
15.	Goalpara	1,008,183	67.37%	964
16.	Morigaon	957,423	68.03%	967
17.	Karbi Anglong	956,313	69.25%	951
18.	Baksa	950,075	69.25%	974
19.	Darrang	928,500	63.08%	954
20.	Kokrajhar	887,142	65.22%	959
21.	Udalguri	831,668	65.41%	973
22.	Nalbari	771,639	78.63%	949
23.	Bongaigaon	738,804	69.74%	966
24.	Dhemaji	686,133	72.7%	953
25.	Hailakandi	659,296	74.33%	951
26.	Chirang	482,162	63.55%	969
27.	Dima Hasao	214,102	77.54%	932

ASSAM LITERACY RATE - CENSUS 2011

The total literacy rate of Assam is 72.19% which is less than average literacy rate 72.98% of India. Also the male literacy rate is 77.85% and the female literacy rate is 66.27% in Assam.

	Assam	India
Female	66.27%	64.63%
Male	77.85%	80.88%
Total	72.19%	72.98%

POPULATION OF ASSAM IN 2017

The total population of the state was 26.66 million with 4.91 million family units in 2001. Higher population fixation was recorded in the areas of Kamrup, Nagaon, Barpeta and Cachar. The population was assessed at 28.67 million in the year 2006, 30.57 million in 2011 and is expected to achieve 34.18 million by 2021 and 35.60 million by the year 2026.

Talking about population, in order to check out the population of Assam in 2017, we need to have a look at the population of the past 5 years. They are as per the following:

1. 2012 – 30.94 Million
2. 2013 – 31.86 Million
3. 2014 – 32.28 Million
4. 2015 – 33.4 Million
5. 2016 – 33.9 Million

Taking a look at the population of Assam from the year 2012-16, it has been noticed that there has been an increase of 2.96 Million in the past 5 years. Therefore, it has been seen that every year the population increases by 0.592 Million. Hence, the population of Assam in 2017 is forecasted to be 33.9 Million + 0.592 Million = 34.492 Million. So, the population of Assam in the year 2017 as per estimated data = 34.492 Million.

Assam Population 2017– 34.492 Million(Estimated)

DEMOGRAPHY OF ASSAM

The Assamese Hindus are the biggest community in the state. The number of inhabitants in Assamese Hindus in Assam is 11,379,000, comprising of 36.50% of the state's population at 2011 evaluation. The People of India venture has contemplated 115 of the ethnic groups in Assam. (69%) distinguish themselves regionally, 22 locally and about 3 trans-nationally. The early pioneers were Austroasiatic and Dravidians speakers, trailed by Tibeto-Burman, Indo-Aryan speakers. Forty-five dialects are spoken by various groups, including three noteworthy dialect families: Austroasiatic (5), Indo-European (12) and Sino-Tibetian (24). Three of the languages doesn't fall in these families.

7 Art and Culture

The culture of Assam is traditionally a hybrid one, developed due to cultural assimilation of different ethnocultural groups under various politico-economic systems in different periods of history. People of Assam are a mixture of Mongolian, Indo-Burmese, Indo-Iranian and Aryan origin. This mixture of people constitutes the population of the state and they call themselves as "Asomiya"' or "Assamese"' and the language is also referred by the same.

The cultural life of Assam basically revolves around the activities of the two most important cultural and religious institutions called the 'Satra' (the seat of the religious head) and the 'Naamghar' (community prayer hall) where the Hindu Vaishnavites (who do not believe in idol worship) recite the name of God by performing 'Naamkirtans'.

Naamghar

Naamghar is a community prayer hall where the Vaishnavite Hindus of Assam recite the name of God. It was introduced in Assam by the Vaishnavite saint Sankaradeva for Assamese people where they can culture and practice naam (devotional songs) and Bhakti of God (devotion). In the Assamese language, *'Naam'* means *prayer and 'Ghar'* means house. Hence, it is called Naamghar. Medhi, Bujandar, Bayan, Namgharia, Bilonia, etc., are some of the officials of *Naamghar.* They are held in high esteem and are respected by the people.

Religious and Social Importance :

A Naamghar is not only a place of worship, but is also a centre of learning, an institution for imparting education, a community hall where people gather to discuss their social problems, a training centre of arts and crafts and above all, a centre of unity of the society.

Satra

Satra is a institutional centers associated with the Ekasarana tradition of vaishnavism, established by the great saint of Assam, Srimanta Sankardeva, with a view to preach Vaishnavism in an organised manner. A Satra works both as the seat of religious learning, as well as, residential schools. The main building of a Satra consists of *Naamghar* or *Kirtan*

Ghar, Karapat, Hati (a quarter for 'Bhakats') and the Satradhikar or Mahanta's residence.

FESTIVALS

Assam is a land of fairs and festivals. The people of Assam enjoy each and every festival to the fullest, irrespective of caste, creed and religion.

Bihu is the chief festival of Assam and it is largely based on agriculture. Bihu is observed with great zeal and enthusiasm by the Assamese people. The traditional Gamocha (a towel woven in cloth) and the unique Bihu dance reflect the richness of the Assamese culture. The people of Assam celebrate three Bihus in a year,namely- the Bohag Bihu, Kati Bihu and Magh Bihu. It is an interesting fact to note that,each Bihu marks a distinctive phase in the farming calendar.

Bohag Bihu is the most colourful and this is why, it is often called as Rongali Bihu. The Bohag Bihu marks the advent of the sowing season and is basically celebrated as the spring festival. The charm of this festival is the unique and graceful Bihu dance.

Kati Bihu is celebrated during the Assamese month of Kati. This Bihu is often called as Kongali Bihu because there is scarcity of crops during the period of this festival.

Magh Bihu is basically the harvest festival of Assam. It is also called as Bhogali Bihu because the celebration of this Bihu is mostly centered around community feast. The most significant part of this Bihu are the huge bonfires called 'Meji' around which, people gather on the eve of Bihu and feast.

Ambubachi Mela

Is the most important festival of Kamakhya temple of Guwahati and is held every year during monsoon (mid-June). It is a ritual of austerities celebrated with 'Tantric rites'. During Ambubashi the doors of the temple remain closed for three days. It is believed that the earth becomes impure for three days. During this time no farming work is undertaken. Ambubachi mela is held at the Kamakhya temple, after being closed for the afore-mentioned three days. On the fourth day only the devotees are allowed to enter inside the temple for worship. Thousands of devotees from all over the country and abroad visit this mela.

Me-Dum-Me-Phi

The most important festival of Ahom. It is celebrated annually at some common venues. It is mainly about worshipping the ancestors. Devotees dressed in traditional fineries take out colourful processing on the occasion.

Baishagu

This festival celebrated in Assam with much pomp and enthusiasm in all over the north east India. This festival is commonly celebrated by the tribe of 'Boro Kacharis' of Assam and it is the famous festival of the Boros. On the first day of Baishagu the cow is worshipped and on the following day young people of each household reverentially bow down to their parents and elders. The Bodos also celebrate Baishagu as a springtime festival at the advent of the new year. In this festival of Baishagu many traditional musical instruments are used. Such music instruments are: Khawbang, Jotha, Gogona, Siphung, Kham etc.

Rongker and Chomangkan

These are the two most important festivals celebrated by the karbis of Assam. The Rongker is besically a spring festival whereas, Chomangkan is the festival dedicated to the dead. It is primarily a death ceremony. Although, the Karbis perform the funeral ceremony at the time of the cremation of the deceased, they also perform the death ceremony called "Chomangkan" at a later date for the eternal peace of the deceased.

Ali Ai Ligang

It is the main festival of the ethnic Mishing community of the region, in which they perform traditional rituals and dances. This festival is celebrated on the first Wednesday of the Phagun month (mid February). The name of the festival is made up of three terms, 'Ali', root and seed, 'Ai', fruit and 'Ligang', to sow.

Some Tribal Festivals of Assam

Festivals		Tribes
• **Ali-Ai-Ligang**	:	Mishings
• **Botiaggiyo Bishu**	:	Deoris
• **Baikho**	:	Rabhas
• **Baishagu**	:	Bodo Kacharis
• **Chomangkan**	:	Karbis
• **Harni Gabra**	:	Dimasas
• **Rongker**	:	Karbis
• **Rajni Gabra**	:	Dimasas
• **Tusu Puja**	:	Tea tribes

(DANCE)

It is often said that folk dance is the best manifestation of the culture and tradition of a particular place. The best example to this statement can be seen in the various ethnic dance forms that are prevalent in the different corners of Assam. The different dance forms in the state can be broadly categorized under two headings, classical dances and folk dances.

Classical Dance

Sattriya is a renowned classical dance of Assam, which was introduced by Srimanta Sankardev to propagate the religion of Vaishnavism.

Ojha-Pali

Ojhapali is an ancient musical art of Assam, which consists of song, drama and dance. Here the Ojha (the lead artist) perform the art form with the help of some Pali (team of performers).The performance is based on tales from Epics and Puranss. The songs are based on raga which are similar with the Chajya Pada. At a time Ojha-pali was the main source of entertainment in different ceremonial functions and festivals of lower Assam.

Bhaona

This dance form is basically performed in the village Namghars and Satras, in order to promote the Vaishnavite culture in Assam. It is actually a theatrical depiction of the one-act play Ankiya Nat, initiated by Sankardeva. An basic part of the dance is the Sutradhara, who recites the Slokas, sings, dances and explains the various stages of Bhaona in detail. Another form of dance included in Bhaona is the Natuwa or Cali dance. One of the subdivisions of this dance form is the Hajowaliya, which is basically a woman's dance and is the combination of both Tandava and Lasya.

(Folk Dance)

Bihu dance

Bihu is the most popular folk dance of Assam and as the very name suggests, is related to the Bihu festival, which is celebrated with much pomp and glory throughout the state. Bihu dances are extremely energetic and performed by young boys and girls. The dances are characterized by brisk steps, stylish footwork, the flinging and waving of hands.

Jhumar Nach

Jhumar Nach was developed over the years by the tribes living and working in the tea gardens, called kulls. It is performed by girls and boys together or sometimes by the girls alone. Boys and girls hold each other's waist and dance to the tunes of the Jhumar dance, with exact precision of foot work. Watching them sway to the tunes of the song is indeed a very pleasant experience.

Deodhani

Deodhani is a dance form associated with the worship of the snake Goddess Manasa. Deodhani Dance is performed only by womenfolk. It is danced as a solo or group performance. The group generally comprises of three to four females. This form of dance is furious and dreadful and is sometimes even called as 'Bhawani Charai' meaning influence of Bhawanimai on women.

Barpeta's Bhortal Nritya

Barpeta's Bhortal Nritya is one of the popular traditional dances of Assam which was developed by a well known Sattriya artist Narahari Burha Bhakat. This dance is performed in a group. Six or seven dancers generally present the Bhortal dance of Assam together. This dance can be performed in larger groups as well. It is performed to a very fast beat. This beat is known as ' Zhiya Nom'. The dancers are equipped with cymbals while performing this dance. This is the uniqueness of this dance from of Assam.

Ornaments

The male and female folk of Assam are not only blessed with a delicate style of dressing but also with beautiful and exclusive ornaments which are basically made of gold and silver.

The traditional ornaments worn by the menfolk of Assam are Biri, Magardana, Motamoni, Kundal and Lokaparo and the traditional ornaments worn by the womenfolk of Assam are Keru, Kanphul, Kharu, Aangathi, Nalak, Keyur, Kardhani, Baju, Kinkini, Nupur, etc.

Dress

The traditional dress worn by the womenfolk of Assam is called 'Mekhela-Chadar' or 'Riha Mekhela'. Mekhela is a skirt and Chadar is Saree. The Mekhela is a cylindrical cloth, which is pleated around the waist. The Chadar is a long length cloth that has its one end tucked in the upper portion of Mekhela and the rest draped around the rest of the body. The traditional Mekhela Chadar is made from the prestigious 'Muga Silk' which is the peculiarity, as well as, the pride of Assam.

The traditional dress worn by the menfolk of Assam is Suria or Dhoti which is tied round their waist. The upper part of the body is covered by

'Kameez' or shirt and over it, a Chadar, known as 'Seleng' is spread by the menfolk of Assam.

(FOOD)

Rice

Rice or Bhaat is the staple food crop of Assam and is also the chief constituent for the production of some unbelievable palatable items like, *Muri, Aakhoi, Chira, Sandah, etc.* Pitha a kind of rice cake, makes an integral food item of the Assamese plate during the Bihu festival and other major occasions. The most lovable and relishable food item among the Assamese people is *'Khar'* which is a reddish curry seasoned with alkali. Fish, especially with a mild sour curry is also a favourite dish of the Assamese people. In Upper Assam, *'Kharisha'* a kind of pickle prepared from bamboo shoots, is vastly consumed. *Kharoli* is another favourite food item of the Assamese people.

Tamul Pan and Assam

Tamul Pan is an essential part of the Assamese society. It holds a significant position in the Assamese culture. *Tamul Pan*, as it is popularly known, is a combination of two ingredients namely, Tamul which implies *areca nut* or *betel nut* and Pan which means *betel leaf. Tamul Pan*, after meal, is a must for every Assamese and is also served to each and every guest.

(ART AND CRAFT)

Art and Craft

Assam has a rich tradition in art and craft. The most striking thing about the arts and crafts of Assam is that they are exactly the way they were even decades ago. The style and the method of production have not changed a single bit in this part of India. The state is significantly rich in various craftsman works in some places of the state which are well known in all over the country. History tells us that the artists and artisans of Assam were known far and wide, for their exquisite craftsmanship. In addition to the world-famous famous silk products, bamboo and cane products have also occupied an important place in handicraft industry of the state. Then, there are the traditional masks, metal handicrafts, paintings, and so on.

Cane and Bamboo

Cane and bamboo are the two most commonly-used materials in daily life in Assam and are used to make a variety of products. Cane and bamboo furniture of Assam in much sought after both in domestic as well as international markets. The Japi, the traditional sun-shade continues to be the most well-known of bamboo items. It has been in use since the days when the great Chinese traveller, Hiuen Tsang came to Assam. Visitors were welcomed with japi(s), decorated with colourful designs and motifs.

Handloom Weaving

Assam is the home of several types of skills,the most prominent and prestigious being Muga, the golden silk exclusive only to this state. There are other forms of silk as well like Eri, and Pat. Assam also has the largest number of weavers in the country. Assam has a long tradition of weaving cloths. In fact, it is a way of life in many parts of the state even today. Most households in villages possesses a loom in which they weave cloths out of cotton and many kinds of the famous Assam silk namely, 'Pat' and 'Muga'. They mostly create 'Mekhela-Chaddar' (a kind of sari worn by Assamese ladies), 'Gamosa' (towels) and other things by weaving.

Masks

With the tribal art and folk elements forming the base of Assamese culture, masks have found an important place in the cultural activities of the people. Masks have been widely used in folk theaters and 'Bhaonas', with the materials ranging from terracotta to pith to metal, bamboo and wood. In the Bhaonas, masks are a must; especially for those playing the parts of mythological characters like 'Hanuman', 'Ravana', 'Garuda', 'Jatayu' etc. and these are made from different materials varying from place to place.

Jewellery

Gold has always constituted the most-used metal for jewellery in Assam, while the use of silver and other metals too have been there for centuries. Gold was available in many of the rivers flowing down from the Himalayas. Jorhat in Upper Assam is one place where the traditional Assamese form of manufacture of jewellery is still in vogue. The typical Assamese jewellery includes several kinds of lockets called as 'Jon-biri', 'Dhol-biri', etc. It also includes bracelets called as 'Gaam-kharu' and necklaces called as 'Gal-pata' and several kinds of earrings.

Pottery

Pottery is probably as old as human civilisation itself. In Assam Pottery is practiced by two communities of artisans the Hira and the Kumar. The Hiras make household articles using the compression method while the Kumars use the wheel to produce his pots.

Terracotta

In the Dhubri district of Assam the terracotta activity is practiced widely in the village of Asharikandi. The people of this village have been practicing terracotta down through several generations. Today we have the descendants of families engaged in improvised terracotta versions of various common figures from gods and goddesses to mythological characters, while toys, vases, etc have also found a new life.

Toys

The toys of Assam have been broadly classified under four categories:

- Clay toys
- Pith
- Wooden,Bamboo toys
- Cloth, cloth-and-mud toys

Clay toys are mainly made in the Goalpara region of Assam and have the characteristic pinched facial rendering of the mother and the child. Besides these, figures of gods, goddesses, and animals are also used by the traditional toy makers. Wood and bamboo have been used for toy making for a long time. These toys are generally used for puppet shows and come in a variety of figures, like birds, animals, and even human forms. The toys made of cloth, or a mixture of cloth and mud, have also become a part of the Assamese toy making culture. Assamese toys made from cloth, so much that it is almost mandatory for every Assamese girl to learn the craft of making cloth toys and the skill is then passed down from one generation to the other.

Presidents, Places and years of the Asom Sahitya Sabha Conventions :

Year	Place/Location	Presidents	Year	Place/Location	Presidents
1917	Sibsagar	Padmanath Gohain Baruah	1971	Makum	Tirtha Nath Sarma
1918	Goalpara	Chandradhar Baruah	1972	Dhubri	Hem Baruah
1919	Barpeta	Kaliram Medhi	1973	Rangiya	Giridhar Sarma
1920	Tezpur	Hemchandra Goswami	1974	Mangaldoi	Dr Maheswar Neog
1923	Jorhat	Amrit Bhushan Devadhikari	1975	Titabar	Dr Satyendranath Sarma
1924	Dibrugarh	Kanak Lal Baruah	1976	Tihu	Jagyeswar Sharma
1925	Guwahati	Lakshminath Bezbaruah	1977	Abhayapuri	Chayad Abdul Malik
1926	Nagaon	Rajanikanta Bordoloi	1978	Golaghat	Prasannalal Choudhuri
1927	Dhubri	Benudhar Rajkhowa	1979	Sualkuchi	Atulchandra Baruah
1928	Goalpara	Tarunram Phukan	1980	Raha	Jatindranath Goswami
1929	Jorhat	Kamalakanta Bhattacharya	1981	Tinsukia	Sitanath Brahma Choudhuri
1930	Golaghat	Mofijuddin Ahmed Hazarika	1982	Diphu	Sitanath Brahma Choudhuri
1931	Sibsagar	Nagendra Narayan Choudhury	1983	Bongaigaon	Dr Birendra Kumar Bhattacharya

Year	Place/Location	Presidents	Year	Place/Location	Presidents
1933	North Lakhimpur	Jnyanadabhlram Baruah	1985	Bihpuria	Jugesh Das
1934	Mangaldoi	Ananda Chandra Agarwalla	1986	Kampur	Biren Barkotoki
1936	Tezpur	Raghunath Choudhury	1987	Pathsala	Dr Mahendra Borah
1937	Guwahati	Krishnakanta Handique	1988	Hailakandi	Kirtinath Hazarika
1940	Jorhat	Maidul Islam Bora	1989	Doomdooma	Mahim Borah
1944	Sibsagar	Nilamoni Phukan	1990	Bishwanath Chariali	Navakanta Baruah
1947	Dibrugarh	Nilamonl Phukan	1991	Dudhnoi	Dr Nirmalprabha Bordoloi
1950	Margherita	Ambikagiri Raichoudhury	1992	Goreswer	Lakhiydhar Choudhuri
1953	Shillong	Surjya Kumar Bhuyan	1993	Sibsagar	Dr Bhupen Hazarika
1954	Jorhat	Nalini Bala Devi	1994	Marigaon	Dr Lila Gogoi
1955	Guwahati	Jatindranath Duwarah	1995	Sarthebari	Hitesh Deka
1956	Dhubri	Benudhar Sharma	1996	Bokakhat	Dr Lakhinandan Borah
1958	Tinsukia	Padmadhar Chaliha	1997	Bilasipara	Dr Nagen Saikia
1959	Nagaon	Atulchandra Hazarika	1998	Haoraghat	Dr Nagen Saikia
1960	Palasbari	Tralyakya Nath Goswami	1999	Hajo	Dr Chandra Prasad Saikia
1963	Nazira	Ratnakanta Borkakati	2001	Dibrugarh	Homen Bargohain
1964	Digboi	Mitradev Mahanta	2003	Lakhimpur	Dr Birendranath Dutta
1965	Nalbari	Dimbeswar Neog	2005	Sipajhar	Kanak Sen Deka
1966	North Lakhimpur	Binondo Chandra Baruah	2007	Chapar	Kanak Sen Deka
1967	Dibrugarh	Nakulchandra Bhuyan	2009	Dhemaji	Rangbong Terang
1968	Tezpur	Jgyanath Borah	2011	Dergaon	Rangbong Terang
1969	Barpeta	Anandachandra Baruah	2012	Ledo	Rangbong Terang
1970	Dhing	Upen Chandra Lekharu	2013	Barpeta	Imran Shah
			2014	Guwahati	Imran Shah
			2015	Kaliabor	Dr Dhrubajyoti Borah

8 Wildlife of Assam

Assam has a rich and wide variety of flora and fauna. One can find a proper admixture of both the Indian and the Malayan species in the wildlife of Assam. It consists of many important and peculiar animals, some of which are found only within the state. It is said that Assam provides shelter to almost more than 189 species of mammals, near about more than 90 species of reptiles, more than 900 species of birds including migratory birds and about 130 species of fishes. Assam has, as many as, 180 species of butterflies.

National Parks and Wildlife Sanctuaries :

NATIONAL PARKS

Name	Area in sq. km	Main Attraction
Dibru-Saikhowa National Park	340.00	Ferel horses, Asiatic Wild Buffalo, White winged wood duck and Salix swamp
Kaziranga National Park	430.00	One-horned rhino, Tiger, Bears, Wild Buffalo, Swamp Deer, Gaur, Gibbon, Bengal Florican, Dolphin, Otter
Manas National Park	500.00	Tiger, Asiatic Wild Buffalo, Asian Elephant, Gaur, Dhole Pigmy hog, Hispid hare, Golden langur, Bengal florican
Nameri National Park	200.00	Tiger, 4 species of Hornbill, White Winged Wood duck, Golden Mahaseer
Rajiv Gandhi National Park	78.91	Rhino, Tiger, Maljurias Bengal Florican, Otter

WILDLIFE SANCTUARIES :

Name	Area in sq. km	Main Attraction
Amchang	78.64	Elephant, Gaur, Leopard, Lesser Cats, Slow Loris, Hoolock Gibbon, Capped Langur
Bornadi	26.22	Hispid Hare, Pygmy Hog, Dhole, Elephants, Tiger, Great Pied Hornbill, Peafowl
Borail	326.25	Serow, Himalayan Black Bear, Hoolock Gibbon, Langur, Spectacled Monkey
Burachapori	44.06	Elephants, Tiger, Wild buffalo, Aquatic Birds, Bengal Florican
Bherjan, Borajan-Padumoni	7.22	Hoolock Gibbon, Capped Langur, Pig-tailed Macaque, Slow Loris and Rhesus Macaque, Leopard

Name	Area in sq. km	Main Attraction
Chakrasila	45.50	Golden Langur, Gaur, Sambar, Barking deer
Dehing Patkai	111.19	Elephants, Tiger, Hoolock Gibbon, White winged Wood Duck, Hombills, Rain forests
East Karbi Anglong	222	Gaur, Elephants, Tiger, Sambar, Barking Deer, Lesser Cats, Hoolock, Gibbon, Capped Langur, Wreathed Hornbill,
Garampani	6.05	Elephant, Hot Water Springs
Hollongapar Gibbon	20.98	7 Primates (Hoolock Gibbon, Stump-tailed Macaque, Capped Langur, Pig -tailed Macaque, Assamese Macaque, Slow Loris and Rhesus Macaque), Elephant, Leopard
Laokhowa	70.13	Elephant, Tiger, Asiatic Wild Buffalo, Bengal Florican
Marat Longri	451.00	Tigers, Leopards, Gaur, Elephants, Hoolock Gibbon
Nambor	37.00	Gaur, Elephants, Tiger, Sambar, Barking Deer, Lesser Cats, Hoolock Gibbon, Capped Langur, Wreathed Hornbill
Nambor- Doigurung	97.15	Gaur, Elephants, Tiger, Sambar, Barking Deer, Lesser Cats, Hoolock Gibbon, Capped Langur, Wreathed Hornbill
Pani-Dihing	33.93	Stray Elephants; Birds Paradise
Pobitora	38.80	Rhino, Leopards, Barking Deer, Migratory Birds
Sonai -Rupai	220.00	Elephant, Tiger, Gaur, Dhole, Sambar, White Winged Wood duck
Pobha or Milroy	49.00	Wild water buffalo, Elephant, Migratory birds

9 Some Tourist Places of Assam

Guwahati is a popular city and tourist destination located in the state of Assam**.** In Guwahati you can visit the Uma Nanda Temple which is dedicated to Lord Shiva and Parvati and it is situated on the Peacock Island in the middle of the river Brahmaputra.

Hajo a small town near Guwahati and an ancient pilgrimage site for 3 religions; Hinduism, Islam and Buddhism. People from all faiths live in Harmony and a very friendly atmosphere exists in the town. The most important religious shrines being the Haryagriva Madhab and the Poa Mecca. This place reflect the 'unity in diversity' of Assam.

Haflong is the only hill station of Assam. It serves as the district headquarters of North Cachar Hills. The breathtaking lake called Haflong lake is situated at the heart of the hill station. It is one of the largest natural water bodies of Assam. The lake offers a variety of leisure activities, like boating.

Sualkuchi is one of the largest weaving villages of the world, also called the Manchester of the East. It is a village renowned for its silk production ,Assam produces there unique varieties of silks, golden muga, the white pat and warm Eri. People from all around the world visit to learn about its magnificent history of weaving.

Sibsagar formally known as Rangpur is an important tourist place which is famous for the monuments and historical building of Ahom dynasty. It was the capital of Ahom kingdom. The Ahoms built a few temples in the region, one of the most prominent of which is the Sivadol Temple. The temple is dedicated to Lord Shiva and attracts a lot of devotees on Shiv Ratri. It as a fast growing town and is also an important centre of tea and oil trades.

Tinsukia is the second largest city in Assam after Guwahati. Many prominent shopping malls are there in Tinsukia. Dibru Saikhowa National park one of the biggest National Park in India is situated in Tinsukia.

Dibrugarh is an important town of North-East Assam and North East India. It is a big centre of trade and commerce and noted for its tea,coat and oil production. It also serves as an important centre of culture and education of the state. It is the largest tea exporting town in India.

Majuli is the largest river island in the world. Nestled in the lap of mighty Brahmputra. It is one of the best place to watch migratory birds,various flora and fauna, green tea gardens and also to experience its culture.

Tezpur is one of the most beautiful town of the state. It is situated on the bank of the mighty Bhramputra has many tourist places like the Da-Parbatia, Bamuni Hills, Chitralekha Park, Agnigarh hills, the Ouguri hills, the Mahabhairav temple etc.

Assam State Zoo cum Botanical Garden is popularly known as Guwahati Zoo. It is located within the Hengrabari Reserved Forest at Guwahati. This zoo acts as homeland to more than 895 reptiles, birds and animals which represent approximately 113 species of birds and animals all over the world. This Zoo attracts many visitors from all over the country as well as from abroad.

Kaziranga National park is one of the oldest national park in Assam. It is famous for one-horned rhinos and composes of up to one third of their world population. The park also abide wild water buffaloes, elephants and different species of birds, reptiles and amphibians. Kaziranga has richness in flora, Grassland and damps are some of the common attributes of the place. Kaziranga National Park has two types of safaris-Jeep Safari and Elephant safari.

State museum came to existence in the 20th century. Some of the finest metal works of the earlier days are stored in this place. The collections here display the rich cultural heritage of the state of Assam. It is the place where you can realize the diversity of the Assamese culture. This museum of Assam is located in the city of Guwahati.

Rang Ghar is two-story oval shape pavilion. It was built by the king Pramatta Singha. It is said that the kings of the Ahom dynasty used to watch different sports from here. During the early days the Rang Ghar of Assam was mainly used for watching elephant fights.

Guwahati Planetarium is an important center for scientific and astronomical studies. The aim of this Planetarium is to spread awareness about astronomy. It is also provide information about the universe along with the several unsolved mysteries and queries. There are regular shows depicting the planetary movements and other astronomical details that attract visitors of all age groups. These shows are held regularly and are very enriching as well.

Cole Park is one of the most beautiful places in Tezpur. The park has two massive ornamented stone pillars, and the sculptural remnants of the famous Bamuni Hills. It was established by a British Deputy Commissioner, Mr. Cole.

Kamakhya Tample located on the Nilachal hills about 800 feet above the sea level in western part of Guwahati city of Assam. It is one of the most famous temples of the state dedicated to Goddess Kamakhya. Devotees from different parts of India and abroad come to visit this temple.

Nabagraha Temple is a popular temple in Assam. Among the temples in India, the Nabagraha Temple is an important one, as it is associated with the ancient studies in India. The Temple is situated in the south-eastern parts of the Guwahati on the crest of the hill known as Citrachala. There are nine Lingas inside the Nabagraha Temple that represent the nine planets or Grahas of Venus, Jupiter, Mars, Saturn and other planets. The two other planets of Ketu and Rahu were added later to this group of planet.

Asvakranta Temple is situated in North Guwahati, the Temple is an important shrine of Assam. It is believed that Shri Krishna Camped here army his army before he defeated and killed Narakasura.

Sukreswara Temple is dedicated to Lord Shiva and is famous for being the abode of the sixth Jyotirlinga of India. The temple is located on the Sukreswar hill or Itakhuli hill by the bank of the mighty Bhramputra River. The temple has one of the largest Shivalingas in India.

Umananda Temple is situated at Peacock Island in the middle of the mighty Bhramputra River. Among the temples in Assam, this temple is one of the mostly visited one. During the Hindu festival of Shivaratri, every year the devotees from all parts of Assam and other parts of India come to this place to pay homage to Lord Shiva.

Mahabhairav Temple is located at Tezpur town, is the oldest and one of the most magnificent holy shrines of Assam. It is believed that the original temple was made of stone, constructed by Banasura, the demon king who had his capital at Tezpur. During the festival of Shivratri, a great festival occurs here.

Madan Kamdeva is a temple complex of 24 temples and is popularly known as "Khajuraho of Kamrup". The art in the sculptures in the temples portray expressions of erotic acts which can be or else seen only in the famous Khajuraho temples of Madhya Pradesh. Madan Kamdeva temple is situated at a distance of 40 km from Guwahati.

Hayagriva-Madhav Temple was constructed in 6th century AD by King of Pala dynasty on Manikuta Hill which is 24 km from Guwahati in Kamrup district. It is a popular tourist destination in Assam. A large number of Bhutanese visit this temple of Assam during winter.

Poa-Mecca is the greatest pilgrimage centre of the Muslim in Assam. It is called Poa Mecca because, it is believed that by offering prayer in this mosque, a devotee can achieve on fourth inner peace and enlightenment, of what could be achieved at the holy 'Mecca' of Saudi Arabia.

Doul Govinda Mandir is famous for its Holi celebrations in the month of February - March. It is Situated at the Rajaduar area of North Guwahati, the Doul Govinda Temple is flocked by thousands of people everyday and the crowd reaches its maximum during the Holi.

Shiv Dol Temple is situated on the bank of the Sibsagar tank. The shiv Dol temple occupies an area of four and a half acres. It is not only the tallest Shiva temple in northeast India, but also the highest Hindu temple in the whole of India. The most important festival celebrated in this temple is Mahashivaratri, and devotees from all over India arrive here to offer Puja.

Manas National Park situated in the foothills of Himalaya in the state of Assam. Manas is famous for its population of the wild water buffalo, rare golden Langur and the red Panda. The park is also home to some of the rare wildlife species including one horned rhinos, leopards, clouded leopards and the amazing black panthers.

10 Education

Assam has an impressive track record with education. The overall literacy rate of Assam as per Census 2011 is 72.19%, where the literacy rate of male is 77.85% and female 66.27%. Huge numbers of educational institutions are established here imparting education to the students of entire. The education system in Assam is categorized into school education and college or university education.

The Government of Assam handles the major part of the education; however, there are schools and colleges that are run by private concerns and famous educationists in the state. Assamese is the medium of instruction in the state run schools, whereas English is preferred as the medium of instruction in the private ones and the colleges and universities.

Some Important Educational and Training Institutes in Assam

School/College	Location
Assam Valley School	Tezpur.
Normal School	Jorhat, Silchar, Chatia, Howli, Bongaigaon.
Sainik School	Mornoi (Goalpara)
Cotton College	Guwahati.
B. Barooah College	Guwahati
Darrang College	Tezpur
J. B. College,	Jorhat
Gauhati Commerce College	Guwahati
Handique Girl's College	Guwahati
Sanskrit College	Guwahati, Nalbari
Agricultural College	Jorha, Bishwanth Chariali
Fishery College	Raha (Nagaon)
College of Veterinary Science	Khanapara (Guwahati)
Police Training College	Dergaon

MEDICAL COLLEGE(S)

School/Colleges	Location
Assam Medical College	Dibrugarh
Gauhati Medical College and Hospital	Guwahati
Silchar Medical College	Silchar
Jorhat Medical College	Jorhat
Government Ayurvedic College	Guwahati
Fakhruddin Ali Ahmed Medical College	Barpeta
Dr J. K. Saikia Govt. Homeopathic Medical College	Jorhat
Assam Govt. Homeopathic Medical : College and Hospital	Nagaon
Swahid Jadav Nath Govt. Homeopathic Medical College	Guwahati
Regional Dental College	Guwahati
Institute of Pharmacy, Gauhati Medical College	Guwahati
Institute of Pharmacy, Assam Medical College	Dibrugarh
Institute of Pharmacy, Silchar Medical College and Hospital	Silchar
Home Science College	Jorhat

ENGINEERING AND TECHNOLOGY COLLEGES AND INSTITUTES

School/College	Location
Indian Institute of Technology	Guwahati
National Institute of Technology	Silchar
Jorhat Engineering College	Jorhat
Assam Engineering College	Guwahati
Prince of Wales Institute of Engineering and Technology	Jorhat
NETES Institute of Technology and Science	Mirza
Girijananda Chowdhury Institute of Management and Technology	Guwahati
Royal School of Engineering and Technology	Guwahati
Don Bosco Institute of Technology	Guwahati
College of Aeronautical Engineering	Borjhar
Central Institute of Technology	Kokrajhar
Central Institute of Plastic Engineering and Technology	Changsari (Near Guwahati)

State Polytechnic(s)	Jorhat, Guwahati, Lahowal (Dibrugarh), Tezpur, Silchar, Nagaon, Golaghat
Basic Training Centre	Titabar, Nalbari, Dudhnoi , Rangia, Kokrajhar.
Industrial Training Institute (ITI)	Jorhat, Tinsukia, Nagaon, Guwahati, Tezpur, Silchar, Barpeta, Bongaigaon, Diphu, etc.

UNIVERSITIES

Colleges/University	Location
Gauhati University	Jalukbari (Guwahati)
Dibrugarh University	Dibrugarh
Central University	Tezpur
Assam University	Silchar
Assam Agricultural University	Jorhat
Don Bosco University	Guwahati (Private)
Assam Down Town University	Guwahati (Private)
K.K. Handique State Open University	Guwahati

MANAGEMENT INSTITUTES

Colleges/Institutes	University
School of Management Science	Tezpur University
Department of Business Administration	Gauhati University
School of Management Studies	Assam University
Centre for Management Studies	Dibrugarh University
Assam Institute of Management	Guwahati
North Eastern Regional Institute of Management **(NERIM)**	Guwahati
Girijananda Chowdhury Institute of Management and Technology	Guwahati
Royal School of Business	Guwahati
Institute of Strategic Business Management **(ISBM)**	Guwahati
Darwin School of Business	Guwahati
CKB Commerce College	Jorhat
Gauhati Commerce College	Guwahati
Don Bosco Institute of Management	Guwahati

ARCHITECTURE INSTITUTES

Colleges/University	Location
Guwahati College of Architecture	Guwahati
Royal School of Architecture	Betkuchi, Guwahati

HOTEL MANAGEMENT INSTITUTES

Colleges/University	Location
North East Institute of Management Science (NEIMS) :	Jorhat
Institute of Hotel Management Guwahati (IHM)	Guwahati

11 Famous Personalities

Banudhar Sharma (1894-1981) was an eminent litterateur and a historian of Assam. He was the president of the Assam Sahitya Sabha in 1956. Sharma was honoured with several awards including the Sahitya Akademi Award and the Padma Bhusan.

Bishnu Prasad Rabha (1909- 1969) was not only a famous freedom fighter of Assam, but also a well known poet, dramatist, dancer and an actor. He was a good musician and a music directer also. So he was awarded as the famous "Kalaguru" Award by Sarvapalli Radhakrishnan at Varanashi. His best song was "Rabha Sangeet".

Bishnuram Medhi (1888- 1980) was an efficient politician. In 1950, he became the Chief Minister of Assam. Medhi's contribution for the development and establishment of North Bengal and Assam is unforgettable. He was also appointed as a Governor of Madras from 1959 to 1964.

Dr. Bhupen Hazarika was Born in the remote town of Sadiya of Assam in 1926. He was a poet, music composer, singer, actor, journalist, author and a renowned film-maker of the very highest repute. His remarkable popularity brought him to the legislative Assembly as an Independent member between 1967 to 1972. In 1977, he received the prestigious Padma Shri Award. He was also honoured with Dadasaheb Phalke Award and Padma Bhushan. He was posthumously awarded the Padam Vibhushan in 2012. Dr. Bhupen Hazarika died on November 5, 2011.

Dimbeswar Neog (1899–1966) was a famous Assamese poet, writer and critic of Assamese literature. He was the president of Asom Sahitya Sabha's 32nd Nalbari session. Neog was selected to be the General Secretary of Assam Chatra Sanmelan from 1921 to 1924. During that period he edited the mouthpiece of Chatra Sanmelan 'Janmabhumi' and 'Milan'. He left for heavenly abode in the year 1966.

Fakhruddin Ali Ahmed (1905- 1977) was an eminent politician and a noted personality of Assam. He was the first person of Assam to be the president of India in the year 1974. As a president of India, he made many goodwill visits to friendly countries across the world. He died in 1977.

Gopinath Bordoloi (1890-1950) The first chief minister of Assam. He was a follower of the Gandhian principle of non violence as a political tool. Due to his unselfish dedication towards Assam and its people,he was conferred with the title "Lokapriya" (loved by all). In 1999, he was posthumously conferred 'Bharat Ratna'.

Jyoti Prasad Agarwala was born in 1903 in Tamulbari tea estate of Dibrugarh. The most valuable gift of Jyoti Prasad Agarwala to Assamese world is 'Joymoti', the first cinema. In 1935 the movie 'Joymoti' was released. He is known as the father of Assamese film. People also called him 'Rupkonwar'(prince of beauty). The Rupkonwar of Assam died of cancer in1951.

Keshav Chandra Gogoi was a politician from the Indian National congress. He was the chief minister of Assam from 13th January 1982 to 19th March 1982. He was member of the Assam Legislative Assembly from Dibrugarh constituency. He died in 1998.

Kushal Konwar (1905 -1943) was an Assamese freedom fighter and the only martyr of the Quit India Movement in India. He was a true patriot and follower of Gandhian philosophy of non-violence. Though he was not directly involved, British hanged Kushal Konwar in relation to the famous Sarupathar derailment 1942.

Lachit Borphukan (1622-1672) was the greatest hero of 'Saraighat War' He was the son of Momai Tamuli Borborua. The Ahom soldiers defeated the Mughal Army by the initiative of Lachit Borphukan in 1671. He died in the year 1672.

Lakshminath Bejbarua (1868-1938) was a great poet, writer, satirist, playwright and children's literature writer. He composed the state anthem 'O Mor Aaapunar Desh'. His autobiographies are ' Mor Jivan Sowaran', 'Dinlekha', and Patralekha. Lakshminath Bejbarua died in 1938.

Madhabdev (1489-1596) was an important preceptor of Sankardev's Ekasarana Dharma. He was the most favourite and devoted disciple of Srimanta Sankardev. His creation 'Naam Ghoxa' is the most prestigious holy book for every Assamese. Madhabdev died in 1596.

Maniram Dewan (1806-1858) Maniram Dutta Barua, Popularly known as Maniram Dewan. He was one of the first people to establish tea gardens in Assam. He was an Assamese nobleman in British India. He played an active role in the freedom movement of Assam. In 1858 he was hanged by the British for conspiring against them during the 1857 uprising, more commonly known as the Indian rebellion of 1857.

Nalinibala Devi (1898-1977) was a noted Assamese poet and writer, known for nationalistic and mystical poetry. She was honoured with 'Padam Shree' in 1957 and 'Sahitya Akademi Award' in 1968.

Nilamoni Phukan (1880-1978) known as a journalist, freedom fighter, Assamese nationalist and a poet. He was twice elected President of the Assam Sahitya Sabha. In 1931 he joined the editorial staff of the Assamese weekly 'Batori'. When it became a daily 'Dainik Batori' in 1935, Nilamoni Phukan became the first editor of the first daily newspaper in Assamese.

Raghunath Chaudhary (1878-1977) was a prominent poet and literate of Assam. He was also known as ' Bihogi Kavi'. Choudhary's first poem was published in 'Jonaki' magazine. He was also sub-editor of 'Jonaki' for sometime. He was also sub-editor of 'Jonaki' for sometime. He was the president of Tezpur session of Asam Sahitya Sabha in 1936.

Syed Abdul Malik (1991- 2001) best known for his immortal short stories, novels, poems and dramas. He is regarded as one of the foremost writers of Assamese literature. He was awarded with Sahitya Academy Award in 1972, 'Padam shri' in 1984. He became the President of Abhayapuri session of Assam Sahitya Sabha in 1977. Popularly known as 'Sahityacharya', the worthy life of his noted personality of Assam came to an end in 2001.

- **Pen Names with Real Names of Some Noted Personalities of Assam**

PEN-NAME	REAL NAME	PEN-NAME	REAL NAME
• *Aghari*	: **Pramode Kumar Bordoloi**	• *Mamoni Raisom Goswami*	: **Dr Indira Goswami**
• *Ajagar*	: **Syed Abdul Malik**	• *Natun Kripabar*	: **Ratnakanta Borkakoti**
• *Aniruddha Kotoky*	: **Munin Borkotoky**	• *Nirmala Devi*	: **Tirthanath Sarma**
• *Astabakra*	: **Karilalakanta Bhattacharya**	• *Nila Baideu*	: **Nirmalprabha Bordoloi**
• *A Native*	: **Anandaram Dhekial Phukan**	• *Niranjan Phukan*	: **Dr Hiren Goliain**
• *Bhattadev*	: **Boikunthanath Bhattacharya**	• *Nilim Kumar*	: **Hemen Kumar Sarma**
• *Bishnupriya Rabha Thakuria*	: **Bishnuprasad Rabha**	• *Nachiketa*	: **Bhabananda Dutta**
• *Bhabananda Pathak*	: **Dr Banikanta Kakati**	• *Pasupati Bharadwaj*:	**Umakanta Sarma**
• *Bhanunandan Pathak*	: **Dr Surya Kumar Bhuyan**	• *Priya Bandhu*	: **Bhabendranath Saikia**
• *Bholai Sarma*	: **Rajanikanta Bordoloi**	• *Rongmon*	: **Robin Dey.**

PEN-NAME	REAL NAME	PEN-NAME	REAL NAME
• *Bina Baruah*	: **Dr Birinchi Kumar Baruah**	• *Raseswar Hazarika*	: **Pabitra Kumar Deka**
• *Bapchandra Bahagwati*	: **Sarat Chandra Goswami**	• *Rashna Baruah*	: **Dr Birinchi Kumar Baruah**
• *Bihguti Bora*	: **Benudhar Sarma**	• *RanaTamuli*	: **Pranab Tamuli**
• *Charu Dutta*	: **Dinesh Chandra Goswami**	• *Ram Das Goswami*	: **Ratneswar Mahanta**
• *Chitrasen Jakharia*	: **Haliram Deka**	• *Rupchandra Bhagwati*	: **Sarat Chandra Goswami**
• *Dhanbor Kais*	: **Mohim Bora**	• *Swami Abhangananda.*	: **Syed Abdul Malik**
• *Dodai*	: **Kirtinath Hazarika**	• *Sima Dutta*	: **Navakanta Baruah**
• *Endi Khurra*	: **Dr Nagen Dutta**	• *Silabhadra*	: **Reboti Mohan Dutta Choudhury**
• *Ekhud Kakaideu*	: **Navakanta Baruah**	• *Sanjay*	: **Dr Bhabendranath Saikia**
• *Ejon Asomiya*	: **Satyanath Bora**	• *Satyapriyo Pathak*	: **Dr Bhabendranath Saikia**
• *Guru Dutta*	: **Gunabhiram Bora**	• *Saurav Kumar Chaliha*	: **Surendranath Medhi**
• *Hibhor Abhoipuria*	: **Parbatiprasad Baruah**	• *Santanoo Tamuli*	: **Pramode Chandra Tamuli**
• *Kripabar Barbaruah*	: **Lakshminaih Bezbaruah**	• *Sonaram Chand*	: **Hemchandra Baruah**
• *Kerpai Sarma*	: **Binanda Chandra Baruah**	• *Sadananda*	: **Lambodar Bora**
		• *Sri Harsha*	**Ananda Chandra Agarwalla**

12 First in Assam

Language and Literature

	Name of the Publication (Year)	By
# First printed book in Assamese	Dharma-Pustak (1813)	Aatmaram Sarma
# First Assamese prose composition	Katha-Gita	Bhattadeva
# First Assamese Grammar	Grammar of the Assamese Language (1839)	William Robinson
# First Assamese printed history	Asom Buranji Puthi (1844)	Kashinath Tamuli Phukan and Radhanath Barbaruah
# First modern play in Assamese	Ram-Navami (1857)	Gunabhiram Baruah
# First Assamese dictionary published	Asomiya Aaru Engraji Abhidhan (1867)	Miles Bronson
# First Assamese poetry to be composed in blank verse	Abhimanyu Badh (1875)	Ramakanta Choudhury
# First modern biography in Assamese	Jiban Charitra (1880)	Gunabhiram Baruah
# First Assamese historical novel	Bhanumati (1890)	Padmanath Gohain Baruah
# First Assamese novel published	Lahori (1892)	Padmanath Gohain Baruah
# First Assamese novel based on the tribal life of Assam	Miri Jiyori (1894)	Rajnikanta Bordoloi
# First Assamese short- story collection	Surabhi (1909)	Lakshminath Bezbaruah
# First history of Assamese literature	Asomiya Sahityar Buranji (1912)	Devendranath Bezbaruah
# First research work on language in Assamese	Asomiya Bhashar Moulik Bichar Aaru Sahityor Chinaki (1912)	Devananda Bharali

	Name of the Publication (Year)	By
# First Assamese bibliography	Asomiya Puthir Talika (Descriptive Catalogue of Assamese manuscripts) (1930)	Hemchandra Goswami
# First Assamese play to be broadcast over AIR	Been Baragi (The Minstrel) (1935)	Prafulla Chandra Baruah
# First Assamese romantic poetry	Bon-Kunwari (The Woodland Nymph)	Chandra Kumar Agarwalla
# First thesis to be written on the Assamese language	Assamese : Its Formation and Development (1940)	Dr Banikanta Kakati
# First Assamese travelogue	Switzerland Bhraman (1948)	Birinchi Kumar Baruah
# First Assamese novel to receive the Sahitya Akademi Award	Yaruyingam (1961)	Dr Birendra Kumar Bhattacharya
# First Assamese book to receive the Sahitya Akademi Award	Banphool (Wild Flowers) (1955)	Jatindranath Duarah
# First Assamese book to be awarded with the Jnanpith Award	Mrityunjoy (1979)	Dr Birendra Kumar Bhattacharya
# First Assamese children's novel	Pataalpuri	Hargovinda Sharma

First In Assam		
• **College**	:	Cotton College (Estd. 1901), Guwahati.
• **University**	:	Gauhati University (Estd. 1948), Guwahati.
• **Private University**	:	Donbosco University (Estd. 2008), Guwahati.
• **Medical College**	:	Assam Medical College (Estd. 1947), Dibrugarh.
• **Film Studio**	:	Jyoti Chitraban (Estd. 1968).
• **High Court**	:	Gauhati High Court (Estd. 1948), Guwahati.
• **Mental Hospital**	:	Lokopriya Gopinath Bordoloi Memorial Mental Health Institute, Tezpur.
• **Radio Station**	:	Guwahati and Shillong (Estd. 1948).
• **Journal**	:	Orunodoi (1846-1882).

• **Assamese Film**	:	Joymati (1935).
• **Assamese Colour Film**	:	Bhaiti (1972)
• **Daily English Newspaper**	:	The Assam Tribune (1946-till date).
• **Printing Press**	:	Mission Press (1844), Sivsagar.
• **Lok Adalat**	:	Hajo (12 Dec. 1987).
• **Children's Magazine**	:	Lora Bandhu (1888).
• **Women's Magazine**	:	Ghar Jeuti (1927).
• **Assamese Modern Drama**	:	Ram-Navami (1857).
• **Assamese Printed Book**	:	Dharma Pustak (1813).
• **Assamese Cartoon Film**	:	Parinam (1989).
• **Bridge Over Brahmaputra**	:	Saraighat Bridge (1962), Guwahati.

First Assamese From Different Fields

Male

• **Assamese Lexicographer**	:	Jaduram Dekabaruah (1839)
• **Chief Minister**	:	Gopinath Bordoloi (1938-39)
• **Chief Justice of Gauhati High Court**	:	Haliram Deka
• **Doctor of Philosophy(Ph.D.)**	:	Maidul Islam Bora
• **D. Litt of London University**	:	Surya Kumar Bhuyan
• **Election Commissioner**	:	Harishankar Brahma (2010)
• **Film-maker**	:	Jyoti Prasad Agarwalla
• **Governor**	:	Bishnuram Medhi (Madras, 1957)
• **Graduate**	:	Anundoram Baruah
• **Honoured with Padma hushan**	:	Bimala Prasad Chaliha
• **I.A.S.**	:	Achyut Saikia
• **I.C.S.**	:	Anundoram Baruah
• **Justice of Supreme Court**	:	Parbati Kumar Goswami
• **President of India**	:	Dr Fakhruddin Ali Ahmed
• **President of Asom Sahitya Sabha**	:	Padmanath Gohain Baruah
• **Recipient of Arjuna Award**	:	Bhogeshwar Baruah (1966)
• **Recipient of Sahitya Akademi Award**	:	Jatindranath Duarah (Banphool), 1955
• **Recipient of Jnanpith Award**	:	Dr Birendra Kumar Bhattacharya (Mrityunjoy), 1979
• **Recipient of National Gramshree Award, 2002**	:	Mridul Deka.
• **Recipent of Padma Vibhushan Award**	:	Dr Bhupen Hazarika (posthumously in 2012)
• **Recipient of Dada Saheb Phalke Award**	:	Dr Bhupen Hazarika (1992)
• **Recipent of Assam Ratna Award**	:	Dr Bhupen Hazarika (2009)
• **Speaker of Assam Legislative Assembly**	:	Babu Basanta Kumar Das (7.4.1937 - 11.3.1946)
• **Vice-Chancellor of Gauhati University**	:	Krishna Kant Handique

Female

• **A.C.S.**	:	Suchibrata Raichoudhury
• **Chief Minister**	:	Syeda Anowara Taimur (1980-81)
• **Doctor**	:	Rajaniprabha Saikia
• **Film Actress**	:	Aaideu Handique
• **Graduate**	:	Sudhalata Duarah and Sukhalata Duarah
• **Honoured with Padma Shri**	:	Nalinibala Devi
• **I.A.S.**	:	Parul Das
• **Justice of High Court**	:	Meera Sarma
• **Minister in the Union Cabinet**	:	Renukadevi Borkotoky
• **MLA**	:	Ms Usha Borthakur, 1952
• **President of Asom Sahitya Sabha**	:	Nalinibala Devi
• **Recipient of Arjuna Award**	:	Monalisha (Baruah) Mehta, 1987
• **Recipient of Jnanpith Award**	:	Dr Mamoni Raisom Goswami (2000)
• **Recipient of Assam Ratna Award**	:	Dr Mamoni Raisom Goswami (posthumously in 2013)

First in Assamese Theatre and Cinema

Theatre :

- **First person to introduce theatre or stage drama in Assam** : Srimanta Sankardeva.
- **First Assamese play to be staged** : Cihnayatra(1468 A.D.), By: Srimanta Sankardeva.
- **First mobile theatre Company** : Nataraj Theatre (1963-64).
- **First Assamese drama to be staged on a revolving stage at Calcutta** : Matir Manuh (1946).
- **First musical drama in Assamese** : Jayadrath Badh (1909), By: Ambikagiri Raichoudhury.
- **First person to introduce co-acting on stage** : Brajnath Sarma (1933), (Troupe : Union Kohinoor Opera Party).

Cinema :

- **First Film maker of Assamese Film** : Aaideu Handique
- **First Assamese Film Director** : Jyoti Prasad Agarwala
- **First female Film Director of Assam** : Suprabha Devi
- **First Assamese Film Studio** : Jyoti Chitraban (Estd. 1934)

First Assamese movie	:	Joymati (1935) (Dir : Jyoti Prasad Agarwala).
First Assamese coloured movie	:	Bhaity (1972) (Dir : Kamal Narayan Choudhury).
First Assamese movie in cinema scope	:	Jeevan Surabhi (1984) (Dir : Naresh Kumar).
First Assamese language thriller movie	:	Dr. Bezbaruah (1969) (Dir : Brajen Baruah).
First full length comedy movie in Assamese film	:	Ito Sito Bahuto (1963) (Dir : Brajen Baruah).
First Assamese children movie	:	Abuj Bedana (1993) (Dir : Gunasindhu Hazarika).
First Assamese broadcast on Doordarshan	:	Brishti (1974) (Dir : Deuti Baruah).
First adult movie	:	Marichika (1972) (Dir : Amulya Manna).
First film to get Swarna Kamal award	:	Halodhiya Charaye Bao Dhan Khai (1987) (Dir : Jahnu Baruah).
First Assamese film to be screened in Indian Panorama	:	Sandhyaraag (1977) (Dir : Dr Bhabendranath Saikia).
First Assamese film dubbed from Hindi	:	Bhagya (1968) (Dubbed from Hindi movie, Taqdeer).
First Assamese film to be screened outside India at the Berlin Film Festival	:	Puberun (1959) (Dir: Prabhat Mukherjee).
First film to be awarded 'National Award' for best script	:	Agnisnan (1985) (Dir : Dr Bhabendranath Saikia).
First Assamese film having a song sung by a non-Assamese singer	:	Era Bator Sur, ('Jonakore Rati Asomire Mati' was the song sung by Melody Queen Lata Mangeshkar).
First Assamese to win Best Film Critic Award at National Film Awards	:	Utpal Borpujari (2003)
First Assamese Film to win the Nargis Dutta Award for Best Feature Film on National Integration		Aai Kot Nai (2008) (Dir : Manju Borah).

13 Transportation

Assam has a modernized, structured and well designed transport infrastructure, including both public and private transportation services. The state is easily accessible to the rest of India through its well connected Air, Rail and Road network that connects it within the state and the rest of the country.

Air : Assam is well connected with the rest of country through air transport. The Lokopriya Gopinath Bordoloi International Airport at Borjhar in Guwahati is the main airport of Assam. The state has other domestic airports and these are located at Jorhat, Dibrugarh, Tezpur, North Lakhimpur and Silchar.

Rail : Assam is well connected by rail with the whole of India. And also all the major towns in Assam are interconnected with railways. The state has a well established railway system. Some of the important Rail heads in the state are Guwahati, Jorhat, Dibrugarh, Bongaigaon, Lumding, Tezpur, Tinsukia, Silchar, etc. Guwahati falls under the Northeast Frontier Railway Zone of the Indian Railways. Guwahati Junction is the headquarters of the zone. Guwahati Junction is the major station of Assam.

Road : Being the gateway of Northeast India all the important towns and villages in the state of Assam are well connected by road to the rest of India. There are as many as 11 National Highways passing through Assam beside the State Roads. The ASTC (Assam State Transport Corporation) and other transport companies have a good number of buses for transportation by road. Besides that, taxis or hired cars are also available.

India's longest river bridge Dhola-Sadiya Bridge:

- India's longest river bridge, the Dhola-Sadiya Bridge, was inaugurated, May 26, 2017 by Prime Minister Narendra Modi.
- The inauguration marks the occasion of the Central government completing three years in office.
- The three-lane, 9.15 kilometre long bridge is located over river Lohit, a tributary of the Brahmaputra River in Assam.
- The bridge will link Dhola in Assam to Sadiya in Arunachal Pradesh
- It is crucial from the strategic perspective as it is close to the border state of Arunachal Pradesh

• Since the bridge is located at a high-seismic region, it was built using state-of-the-art equipment, including imported hydraulic rigs, and is provided with seismic buffers in all its 182 piers.

• The bridge shall enhance Indian Army's mobilisation capabilities and movement of troops and heavy equipment in the forward areas bordering China. The construction of the bridge began in 2011 at a project cost of Rs 950 crore.

• National Highway Passes Through Assam

NH No.	Route	Length (km.)
31	From W.B. Border-Gouripur-North Salmara-Bijni- Charaliamingaon Junction with NH No.37	322
31B	North Salmaria-Abhayapuri-Junction with NH No37 near Jogighopa	19
31C	From W.B. Border-Kochugaon-Sidli Ju. With NH-31 near Bijni	93
36	Nagaon-Dabaka-Amlakhi-Nagaland Border	167
37	Dispur-Nowgong-Numaligarh-Jorhat-Jhanzi-Dibrugarh-Tinsukia-Makum-Saikhoghat	680
37A	Kuwari Tal – Junction with NH.No.52 near Tezpur	23
38	Makum-Ledo-Likhapani	54
39	Numaligarh-Naojan-Bokajan-upto Nagaland Border	115
44	From Meghalaya Border- Badarpur-Karimgant-Patharkandi- upto Tripura Border	111
51	Paikan-upto Meghalaya Border	22
52	Baihata-Charali-Mangaldai-Dhekiajuli-Tezpur-Gohpur-Bander Dewa- North Lakhimpur-Dhemaji-Kulajan-Arunachal Border-Junction with NH No.37 near Saikhoaghat	540
52A	Gohpur-A.P. Border-Bander Dewa	15
52B	Kulajan-Dibrugarh	31
53	Junction with NH-44 near Badarpur-Silchar-Lakhipur- upto Manipur Border.	100
54	Dabaka-Lumding-Langting-Haplong- Silchar-Dwarband upto Mizoram Border	335
61	Jhanzi-Amguri-Nagaland border	20
62	Dudhnai-Damara- upto Meghalaya Border	5
151	Karimganj-Bangaladesh Border	14
152	Patacharkuchi-Hajua-Bhutan Border	40
153	Ledo-Lekhapani-Arunachal Pradesh Border	20
154	Dhaleshwar (Badarpur)-Bhairabhi -Mizoram Border	110

Source : Union Ministry of Transport and Shipping

- **Road Distance From Guwahati in km**

Guwahati to Major Cities of India			
Places	**Distance (km.)**	**Places**	**Distance (km.)**
• Agartala	599	• Itanagar	389
• Agra	1756	• Jaipur	1961
• Aizawl	466	• Kohima	340
• Bengaluru	2,932	• Kolkata	1151
• Bhopal	1855	• Lucknow	1479
• Bhubaneswar	1483	• Mumbai	2746
• Chandigarh	2145	• Patna	1023
• Chennai	2718	• Ranchi	1206
• Dehradun	2000	• Shimla	2250
• Delhi	1960	• Srinagar	2783
• Gangtok	590	• Thiruvananthapuram	3426
• Hyderabad	2370		
• Imphal	484		

Guwahati to Important Places in Assam			
Places	**Distance (km.)**	**Places**	**Distance (km.)**
• Barpeta Road	137	• Karimganj	338
• Barpeta	140	• Kaziranga	225
• Biswanath Chariali	255	• Kokrajhar	236
• Bongaigaon	210	• Ledo	546
• Dergaon	280	• Lumding	224
• Dhaligaon	199	• Manas	159
• Dhekiajul	137	• Mancachar	269
• Dhemaji (via Bordoloni)	469	• Mangaldai	68
• Dhubri	290	• Morigaon	78
• Dibrugarh	443	• Nagaon	123
• Digboi	527	• Nalbari	71
• Diphu	271	• Namrup	460
• Duliajan	523	• North Lakhimpur	396
• Goalpara	150	• North Salmara	194
• Golaghat	288	• Patacharkuchi	97
• Haflong	388	• Saikhowaghat	537
• Hailakandi	336	• Sivasagar	363
• Hajo	32	• Silchar	343
• Jagiroad	55	• Silghat	185
• Jorhat	308	• Tezpur	181
• Jogighopa	212	• Tihu	99
		• Tinsukia	491
		• Udalguri	131

14 Industry

Industry of Assam

Assam is a house of natural and precious mineral resources. Assam, although, finds its place in the industrially developed map of the world during the pre- independence period, the continuous process of economic and industrial development of the State was almost stopped after attainment of independence and at present Assam is amongst the industrially under- developed states in the Country. Therefore, industrial scenario of the state is confined within the growth of employment oriented SSI (Small Scale Industry)Sector. Assam is still making efforts desperately for gearing up industrial activities by harnessing the un-tapped resources available in the state through various growth-inducing factors as well as by removing the infrastructure inadequacies primarily in the power sector. Despite existence of constraints a favourable industrial climate is gradually being created in the State as discernible from the increasing interest shown by investors both from within the State as well as from outside the State. The communication and transport sector, on the other hand, has shown some improvement during the recent past.

Almost 63% of the society of Assam earns its living from the agriculture sector. The state is reputed all over the world for its tea production. Assam produces more than 50% of India's tea, and is the largest tea growing area in the world. Assam's tea industry employs nearly 800,000 workers who are one of the lowest paid groups in India's organized sector. The meagre daily wage of Rs 126 is far below the state legal minimum of Rs 240 per day.

The performance of annual growth of industrial sector, a combination of Manufacturing, Mining and Quarrying, Electricity Gas, Water Supply and Construction sectors, showed some recovery during the recent years after sudden slow down in the year 2010-11.

The average annual GSDP growth rate from 2004-05 to 2014- 15 was 9.9 percent.

List of locally found raw materials, their area and producible goods in Assam.

Locally found raw material	Where found	Producible goods
Timber (Sal, Bansum, Gamari, Sishu, Sonaru, Titasopa, etc) Simalu	Entire State. Particulary Kamrup, Nagaon, Golpara, Darrang	(a) Railway Sleeper (b) Plywood, Particle Khokan, boards, hard board, etc (c) Building materials. (d) Furniture. (e) Other timbers frames, icons, figures of use like cotton. (f) Paper pulp and fuel
Medical plants (Arjun, Aswagandha, Ashok, Molar, silika, Amlakhi, Bel, Sewali, Jaba, Sarapagardhe, Tetali, Bhoira, Thekere, Salmugra, Olatkambal, Ou, Boku, Jamu Amara, Tulasi, etc. And Hundered of hereds and creepers)	Entire States	(a) Medicinal oil and scent (b) Medicine (c) Fuel
Cane (Raidang, Patidoibet, etc.)	Entire State Particularly Upper Assam and Cachar,	(a) Furniture baskets, chairs etc. (b)Umbrella handle,stick,rope,etc
Bomboo (Bhaluka, jati, kotah, Nal, Kekoa, etc.)	Entire State	(a) Building materials. (b) Utility (domestic and cultivation) goods. (c) Paper pulp, fodder etc.
Other utility plants (khoir, Nahar, Agor, Majankari, Som, Era, Sowalu, Barhamthuri Majathi, Indigo, Bata, Khagari, Kher, Takeu, Tara, etc)	Entire State	(a) Non-edible oil (b) Muga and Eri cocoon rearing (c) Scent and other utility goods, Khoir, gum, dye, Jaju, etc.
Stone, stone chips, Earth and sand	Entire State	(1) Building materials (2) Brick, earthen wares, tiles, etc. (3) Glass, icon, figures, etc

Besides there are 50 to 60 less durable or Akathi timber species in the State and these timbers can be made fit for use in manufacturing frames, boxes,plants, building, etc. with due treatment . So, there is also scope for timber treatment plants in the State .

Castor oil, Nahar oil, Neem seed oil, Agor oil, Menthol and popperuiant oil, seed oil, etc., can be prepared extensively if seeds are properly collected in time . Besides citronella or lenon - grass oil, all the above oils are good foreign exchange earners. Lac, rubber , gum , Katha or Khoir can be extracted from forests and production can be continued and expanded with proper plantation planning . Beside it seems there is no scheme to protect and increase these plantations in the State.

Fruit cultivation, or Preservation and Canning Industry

Assam with a wide range and pineapple are commercially most important for processing. Processing and canning may be extended to other perishable fruits. Pineapples and oranges are cultivated on a commercial scale. Bananas and papayas, and to a small extent pears, plums, peaches, etc., are also grown. Since fruit is perishable in nature it requires careful handing especially during transportation . For the fruit industry to progress on a commercial scale it is necessary to provide quick and easy transport and refrigeration facilities. In Assam , at present , these are fruit preservation centres one each at Guwahati, Silchar , Kuthari (Nagaon) , Dibrugarh , Tinsukia and Jorhat. Fruit cells, peels, seeds and wastes also can be utilised profitably for processing to avoid wastes.

Among the various minerals that may be taken up for investigation to implement the programmes of development are :-

Coal

Detailed providing of low ash coal in the Makum field,

Exploration for coal in the Karbi Anglong district.

Feldspar

Feldspar occur in pegmatites in the Archacean gneissic complex in the Karbi Anglong,North Cachar Hills,Goalpara and Kamrup.

Iron ore

The geological Survey of India has intensified the search for metalliferous deposits in Assam. As a result,occurrence of banded magnetic quartzite,similar to the Salem iron ores of Madras,have been found in West Goalpara and along the Kamrup border. The bands on the Chandordinga Hill on the north bank of the Brahmaputra,west of Goalpara and also the one on the hill south of Hahim in Kamrup district are reported to be fairly large.

The proportion of magnetite in the rock is reported at 25 to 30 per cent and the total iron content may be upto 50 per cent.

Gypsum

A gypsiferous shale has been reported in the Disama Reserve Forest in the Karbi Anglong district. In view of the importance of this mineral to the cement industry,which has to be brought from a far as Bikaner in Rajashthan,the investigation of the occurrence assumes great importance.

Salt

Brine springs occur in Bhubhan Hills in Cachar district. Small quantities of salt were extracted from these. However,the sources are small and large scale production cannot be thought of .

Fire-Clay

Fire-Clay occurs in association with coal in the Makum coalfield. Though the reserves have not been estimated so far,the deposit is reported to be large. Besides,a number of clay horizons varying in thickness from 1 to 5 metres are found associated with coal seams near Koilajan. The reserves have not been assessed but according to one source as much as 5-6 million tonnes may be available here. Samples from the horizon at the base of the Sylhet limestone are reported to be promising for high grade refractories. Presence of copper has been reported from Meghalaya hills in Goalpara district. In view of poor copper resources of India,its above occurrence should be investigated further.

Formation of State Government Corporation for Development of Industries :-

In order to formulate suitable infrastructural and follow-up guidance in the sphere of industrial development in the State,the Government set up a number of corporations to work as its agency in respect of functions entrusted to each of them. These are as follows :-

Assam Small Industries development Corporation Ltd. :- This corporation was established in the year 1962 under the Indian Companies Act. The objectives of the Corporation are

(i) To promote,establish and set up small scale industries in the State with a view to transferring any of such small industries ultimately to entrepreneurs who evidence interest and keeness in setting up such small industries,

(ii) To aid,assist,counsel and finance any industrial undertaking with capital,credit and resources,

(iii) To promote,establish,and execute industrial project or enterprise for manufacture and production of various projects

(iv) To promote and operate schemes for small industries,

(v) To procure capital and financial assistance or provide machinery and other facilities for the purpose of establishment of industries and

(vi) To assist small scale industrial units in getting essential raw materials.

The Corporation took over a number of units from the Industries Department to run them commercial basis,one of which is match Splint Factory, Bijni.

The other units are :

- **Assam Ayurvedic Products:-** This units has been successfully manufacturing a wide range of Ayurvedic which have been well received throughout the State.
- **Cachar Textile Industries, Badarpur :-** This unit came up with 196 power looms with a sizing and calendering plant. Besides commercial manufacturing of gray cloth, the unit had also a training unit. After running the unit for about eight years,the power looms have recently been distributed to a number of local entrepreneurs. The Corporation is running the sizing and the calendering plant to help the power loom units run by private entrepreneurs.
- **Distribution of raw materials : -** For distribution of raw materials,the Corporation has depots at Guwahati,Tinsukia,Jorhat,Bongaigaon,Tezpur and Badarpur from where small scale units can get supply of essential raw materials.

Assam Industrial Development Corporation Ltd.: This Corporation was incorporated in the year 1965 with the objectives to promote,establish,assist and finance industrial projects or enterprises,companies and associations for the purpose of development of industries in the State.

In fulfillment of these objectives the Corporation has already taken up the following projects :-

(a) Assam Petro-Chemical Ltd.
(b) Cachar Sugar Mills Ltd.
(c) Fertichem Ltd.
(d) Chemical unit of Associated Industries (Assam) Ltd.
(e) Assam Conductors & Tubes Ltd.
(f) Jute mill at Dalgaon.

In addition to this,the A.I.D.C. Ltd. has participated in the share capital of North Assam Agro Industries Co-operative Society for setting up of a Rice Bran Oil Plant at Rowta in the Darrang district. The Corporation has taken over management of Assam Glass Industries Pvt. Ltd. Besides these industrial units,the Corporation has also obtained a number of licences for industries like.

(i) Manufacture of Cigarettes
(ii) Sponge Iron
(iii) Card Board
(iv) Portland Cement
(v) Carbon Black
(vi) Maize Products
(vii) Cotton Yarn

(viii) Melamine

(ix) Brewery

Some Important Industries

Jute

Assam is one of the famous state of India in respect of Jute production. In assam, a co-operative Jute Mill was established at Silghat of Nagoan district in 1970. The government of Assam has laid foundation store two Jute Mill- One at Mangaldoi and another at Barpeta area.

Match

The first attempt at manufacture of safety matches in the small scale industry in the State was made in 1912 at Sibsagar in the name and style of Rampur Match Factory. But the unit was closed down soon after its birth. The second and biggest attempt was the Brahmaputra Match Factory at Jorhat,which was also closed down almost at its very start. The reason for the failure was perhaps the high cost of production and non-availability of abundant suitable timber near about.

But in 1924,abundance of *simul* timber in Goalpara,Kamrup and Nagaon and imposition of import duty on safety matches by the Government of India,prompted a Swedish Company and set up a match factory at Dhubri.Initially the match factory was known as Assam Company. The name of the company has been now changed to 'WIMCO'.

Cottage

Assam was traditionally famous for its cottage industry,especially spinning and weaving. Pat or pure silk production is especially confined to Assam. The state produces about 10% of total natural silk of India. Assam also produce Muga. The golden weaving is vital cottage industry of Assam.

Brass and Bell Metal

Brass and bell metal products are an important traditional craft form in Assam. The Normal products of Bell metal are the traditional plates, cups,bowls,pots and musical instruments. Brass articles are produced not only for day-to-day life use, but also for interior decoration.

Crude Oil

Assam is a producer of **crude oil** and it accounts for about 15% of India's crude output, exploited by the Assam Oil Company Ltd., and natural gas in India and is the second place in the world (after Titusville in the United States) where petroleum was discovered. Asia's first successful mechanically drilled oil well was drilled in Makum way back in 1867. Most of the oilfields are located in the Eastern Assam region. Assam has four oil refineries in Digboi (Asia's first and world's second refinery), Guwahati, Bongaigaon and Numaligarh and with a total capacity of 7 million metric tonnes (7.7 million short tons) per annum. Asia's first refinery was set up at Digboi and discoverer of Digboi oil field was the Assam Railways & Trading Company Limited (AR & T Co. Ltd.), a registered company of London in 1881. One of the biggest public sector oil company of the country Oil India Ltd. has its plant and headquarters at Duliajan.

Other Industries

There are several other industries, including a chemical fertiliser plant at Namrup, petrochemical industries at Namrup and Bongaigaon, Paper mills at Jagiroad, Hindustan Paper Corporation Ltd. Township Area Panchgram and Jogighopa, Sugar mills at Barua Bamun Gaon, Chargola, Kampur, Cement plant at Bokajan and Badarpur, Cosmetics plant of Hindustan Unilever (HUL) at Doom Dooma, etc. Many of these industries are facing loss and closure due to lack of infrastructure and improper management practices.

15 Natural Resources of Assam

Any matter or energy derived from the environment that is called Natural resource. Assam is rich in natural resources. The Natural resources of Assam are classified into two categories - Renewable resources and Non-renewable resources.

(a) Resources which get renewed and replenished fast are called **Renewable resources.** Land, water, forests, fisheries and power are examples of Renewable resources.

Land Resources: Assam is basically an agriculture dependent state. More than 65 percent of its total area is under agriculture. There are different types of soil in the state. Its soil suits tea cultivation. With 2.39 percent landscape in the country, the state has to cater to the need of 2.92 percent national population.

Water Resources : Assam is endowed with enormous water resources. The large perennial rivers and other water bodies with the rich aquifer speak about vastness of its water resource. Surface water is available in the forms of river, stream, lake, swamps, pond etc. They can be better used for irrigation, power generation and navigational purposes. The Brahmaputra and the Barak rivers together with their tributaries account for 31 percent of India's water resources.

Water Resources play significant role in the economic development of the state :

Water resources are widely used fisheries in the state economy; and they are used for navigational purpose. Meanwhile, the Government announced the waterway, through the Barak and the Brahmaputra, as the national waterway. Newly opened Numligarh Refinery largely uses the waterway of Brahmaputra.

Forest Resources: Assam is famous for its abundant forest resources. A large part of Assam is covered by hills and forests. These hills and forests contain valuable trees in large quantities. Karbi Anglong and

North Cachhar have maximum forest. Currently, there are 611 mills and factories including paper, match and plywood factories which largely depend on the forest products in the state.

Power Resources: The state is generously blessed by nature with its huge power potential based on water, natural gas, coal and oil. It has alone 28 percent of the total hydro power potential of the country. It has also a number of coal based thermal plants to produce electric power.

(b) Non-Renewable Resources are built over a very long geological time. Mineral is an example of **Non-Renewable Resource**s. Assam is largely endowed with many mineral resources, such as crude oil, coal, limestone and natural gas etc. However, the state mineral resources have not yet been completely assessed. These resources feed both industries and power sector of the state. There are four oil refineries in the state. They are at Noonmati (Guwahati), Bongaigaon, Digboi and Numaligarh.

Petroleum: Among the North-East States, Assam along shares nearly 50% of crude oil production of India. Assam is the mother of Indian petroleum industry. In India, petroleum was first discovered in Assam. It was Digboi in Assam where the first Oil Refinery in Asia came up. The crude oil or petroleum sector of the state plays an important role in the economic development of the regional economy.

Coal : Coal is one of the key natural resources of Assam. It is estimated that Assam has about 510 million tonnes of coal reserves. Assam coal have high calorific value, low ash content high percentage of sulphur and low oxygen content. The first coal minings in the region was started in 1865 at the Makum coal-fields by the erstwhile Assam Railway and Trading Company and now it is mined by the North Eastern Coal-Fields. The coal belt extends from Dilli-Joypur in the west to Tipok in the east.

Coal is found in Koilajan, Umrangshu, Khota-Arda in the Hills Districts of Assam and is mined by the Assam Mineral Development Corporation.

Natural Gas : In Assam, almost all the petroleum producing areas of the Brahmaputra valley, especially Naharkatia, Moran, Lakuwa and

Rudrasagar, contains 'associated natural gas'. The important industries so far built up on the basis of the natural gas of Assam are Namrup Fertilizer

Factory, Namrup Thermal Power Project, Production of Carbon Black, Assam Petrochemicals and Assam Gas Company, which provides liquefied petroleum gas for domestic use.

Limestones : In the North Cachar Hills, limestone beds of about 500 to 700 feet thickness and in the Mikir Hills of about 200 feet thickness are found. In fact, limestone feeds the needs of Bokajan Cement Factory as well as other allied industrial units of the country by bringing huge revenue for Assam.

Fisheries : Assam is endowed with vast fishery resources in the form of rivers, ponds, derelict water bodies, beels covering about 2.85 lakh ha. in addition to the two major river system viz. the Brahmaputra and the Barak with their tributaries. Despite high development potential, the state fishery resources are lagging behind in comparison to other states like Orissa, Andhra Pradesh and West Bengal. Fish occupies an important place in the lives of the people of the state and fish farming has been one of the common activities in the rural areas.

16 Awards and Awardees

The state of Assam has been blessed with a number of awardees both at the state and the national level. Let's know some of the awards and their awardees in Assam.

National-Awardees From Assam:

NATIONAL AWARDS	RECIPIENTS	YEAR
• *Padma Bhushan*	**Nabakanta Baruah**	1976
• *Padma Shri*	**Parveen Sultana**	1976
• *Best Composer in India*	**Dr Bhupen Hazarika**	1977
• *Jnanpith Award*	**Dr Birendra Kumar Bhattacharya**	1979
• *Dada Saheb Phalke Award*	**Dr Bhupen Hazarika**	1992
• *Rajiv Gandhi Sadbhavna Award*	**Late Hiteswar Saikia**	1995
• *Padma Shri*	**Dipali Barthakur**	1998
• *Padma Bhushan*	**Pushpalata Das**	1999
• *Bharat Ratna*	**Gopinath Bordoloi (Posthumously)**	1999
• *Bharat Shree*	**Bijit Gogoi**	2000
• *Bharatiya Bhasha Parishad Award*	**Nilamoni Phukan**	2000
• *Ambedkar Award*	**Chetana Das**	2000
• *Jnanpith Award*	**Dr Mamoni Raisom Goswami**	2000
• *Sangeet Natak Akademi Award*	**Arun Sharma, Prabhat Sharma and Koshkanta Dev Goswami**	2003
• *Ambedkar Fellowship Award*	**Swarna Hazarika**	2003
• *Padma Shri*	**Hem Bharali and Kanaksen Deka**	2004
• *Sangeet Natak Akademi Award*	**Khirod Khaklari**	2005
• *National Bravery Award*	**Ratul Chandra Rabha, Rituparno Boro**	2005
• *Kabir Puraskar*	**Md. Aynal Haque**	2005
• *Ajan Peer Award*	**Late Rekibuddin Ahmed**	2005
• *Sangeet Natak Akademi Award*	**Mrs Garima Hazarika, Dharani Barman and Kotitra Sarghiyari**	2006
• *Arjuna Award*	**Jayanta Talukdar**	2006
• *Sangeet Natak Akademi Award*	**Gunakanta Dutta Barbayan**	2007
• *Padma Shri*	**Shri Surjya Kanta Hazarika, Shri Jatin Goswami and Dr (Mrs) Sheela Barthakur**	2008
• *Best Film Critic at 56th National Film Awards 2008*	**Altaf Mazid**	2008
• *Sangeet Ratna*	**Dr Bhupen Hazarika**	2009
• *Padma Shri .*	**Arun Sharma**	2009

NATIONAL AWARDS	RECIPIENTS	YEAR
• *Sangeet Natak Akademi Award*	**Moinul Hoque**	2009
• *Sangeet Natak Akademi Award*	**Mimik Borbayan**	2010
• *Padma Shri*	**Mahim Bora**	2011
• *Padma Vibhushan*	**Late Dr Bhupen Hazarika**	2012
• *Padma Shri*	**Sunil Janah**	2012
• *Padma Shri*	**Ghanakanta Bora Barbayan**	2013
• *Padma Shri*	**Hemendra Prasad Barooah**	2013
• *Padma Shri*	**Mukul Chandra Goswami**	2014
• *Padma Bhushan*	**Jahnu Barua (Art)**	2015
• *Padma Shri*	**Dr Lakshmi Nandan Bora**	2015
• *Padma Shri*	**Jadev Molai Peyang**	2015
• *Padma Shri*	**Dhirendra Nath Bezbaruah**	2016
• *Padma Shri*	**Prahlad Chandra Tasa**	2016
• *Padma Shri*	**Smt. Eli Ahmed**	2017
• *Padma Shri*	**Shri Jitendra Nath Goswami**	2017
• *Padma Shri*	**Shri Prafulla Govinda Baruah**	2018
• *Padma Shri*	**Shri Arup Kumar Dutta**	2018
• *Padma Shri*	**Ms. Joyshree Goswami Mahanta**	2018

• **Srimanta Sankardeva Award :** The government of Assam instituted this prestigious award to honour persons of eminence in the field of Journalism, Art, Culture and Literature in the hallowed name of Mahapurush Srimanta Sankardeva in 1986. The award is given to only individuals of 50 years of age and above. The recipients of this award so far, are :

RECIPIENTS	YEAR	RECIPIENTS	YEAR
• **Kirtinath Hazarika**	: *1986*	• **Ilaram Das**	: *2001*
• **Bhupen Hazarika**	: *1987*	• **Indira Miri**	: *2002*
• **Satyajit Ray**	: *1988*	• **Habib Tanbir**	: *2003*
• **Maheswar Neog**	: *1989*	• **Narayan Chandra Goswami and Parveen Sultana**	: *2004*
• **Kapila Vatsayan**	: *1990*		
• **Satyendra Nath Sarma**	: *1991*		
• **Ramchandra Narayan Dandkar**	: *1992*	• **B. G. Verghese**	: *2005*
		• **Keshavananda Goswami**	: *2006*
• **Satyaprasad Baruah and Gangubai Hangel**	: *1993*	• **Homen Borgohain**	: *2007*
		• **Sharmila Tagore**	: *2008*
• **Mahendra Bora**	: *1994*	• **Kanaksen Deka**	: *2011*
• **Syed Abdul Malik**	: *1995*	• **M. L. Varatdpande**	: *2014*
• **Bhabesh Shanyal**	: *1996*	–	
• **Kelucharan Mahapatra**	: *1997*	–	

RECIPIENTS	YEAR	RECIPIENTS	YEAR
• **Bhabendranath Saikia**	: *1998*	–	
• **Ustad Amjad Ali Khan**	: *1999*	–	
• **Sonaram Chutia**	: *2000*	–	

• **Assam Valley Literary Award :** This yearly award is given by the Williamson Magar Education Trust to honour the eminent writers of Assam. This award was instituted in the year, 1990. The recipients of this award so far, are:-

RECIPIENTS	YEAR	RECIPIENTS	YEAR
• **Bhabendranath Saikia**	: *1990*	• **Dr Lakshmi Nartdan Borah**	: *2004*
• **Homen Borgohain**	: *1991*	• **Arun Sarma**	: *2005*
• **Syed Abdul Malik**	: *1992*	• **Nalinidhar Bhattacharya**	: *2006*
• **Navakanta Baruah**	: *1993*	• **Nagen Saikia**	: *2007*
• **Jogesh Das**	: *1994*	• **Rangbong Terang**	: *2008*
• **Saurav Kumar Chaliha**	: *1995*	• **Imran Shah**	: *2009*
• **Umakanta Sarma**	: *1996*	• **Harekrishna Deka**	: *2010*
• **Nilamoni Phukan**	: *1997*	• **Purabi Bormudoi**	: *2011*
• **Mohim Bora**	: *1998*	• **Sameer Tanti**	: *2012*
• **Ajit Baruah**	: *1999*	• **Atulananda Goswami**	: *2013*
• **Hiren Bhattacharya**	: *2000*	• **Hirendra Nath Dutt**	: *2014*
• **Silabhadra**	: *2001*	• **Apurba Sarma**	: *2015*
• **Chandraprasad Saikia**	: *2002*	• **Arupa Kalita**	: *2016*
• **Nirupama Borgohain**	: *2003*	• **Sananta Tanti, Yeshe Dorjee Thongchi, Dr Rita Chowdhury**	: *2017*

• Sahitya Akademi Award:

Sahitya Akademi Award is given each year, since 1955, by Sahitya Akademi to writers for their noble contributions in the literature. Several Assamese writers have so far received this award. Their names are:

RECIPIENTS	PUBLICATIONS	YEAR
♦ **Jatindranath Duarah**	Bana phul *(Poetry)*	*1955*
♦ **Benudhar Sarma**	Kangrechar Kachiyali Ra'dat *(Reminiscences)*	*1960*
♦ **Dr Birendra K Bhattacharya**	Iyaruingam *(Novel)*	*1961*
♦ **Birinchi Kr. Baruah**	Asomor Loka-Sanskriti *(Study in Folk Culture)*	*1964*
♦ **Ambikagiri Raichoudhury**	Bedonar Ulka *(Poetry)*	*1966*
♦ **Trailokyanath Goswami**	Aadhunik Galpa Sahitya *(Literary Criticism)*	*1967*

RECIPIENTS	PUBLICATIONS	YEAR
♠ **Nalinibala Devi**	Alakananda *(Poetry)*	*1968*
♠ **Atul Chandra Hazarika**	ManchaLekha *(Study of Assamese Theatre)*	*1969*
♠ **Lakshminath Phukan**	Mahatmar Pora Rupkonwarloi *(Reminiscenses)*	*1970*
♠ **Syed Abdul Malik**	Aghori Aatmaar Kahini *(Novel)*	*1972*
♠ **Saurav Kumar Chaliha**	Golam *(Short Stories)*	*1974*
♠ **Navakanta Baruah**	Kokadeutar Har *(Novel)*	*1975*
♠ **Dr Bhabendranath Salkia**	Shrinkhal *(Short Stories)*	*1976*
♠ **Ananda Chandra Baruah**	Bokul Banor Kabita *(Poetry)*	*1977*
♠ **Homen Borgohain**	Pita-Putra *(Novel)*	*1978*
♠ **Bhaben Baruah**	Sonali Jahaj *(Poetry)*	*1979*
♠ **Jogesh Das**	Prithibir Asukh *(Short Stories)*	*1980*
♠ **Nilamoni Phukan**	Kabita *(Poetry)*	*1981*
♠ **Indra Goswami (Mamoni Raisom Goswami)**	Mamore Dhora Tarowal Aaru Dukhon, Upanyash *(Novel)*	*1982*
♠ **Nirmalprabha Bordoloi**	Sudirgha Din Aaru Rati *(Poetry)*	*1983*
♠ **Debendranath Acharya (Posthumously)**	Jangam *(Novel)*	*1984*
♠ **Krishnakanta Handique (Posthumously)**	Krishnakanta Handiquear Rachana Sambhar *(Literary Criticism)*	*1985*
♠ **Tirthanath Sarma**	Benudhar Sarma *(Biography)*	*1986*
♠ **Harekrishna Deka**	Aan Ejon *(Poetry)*	*1987*
♠ **Lakshminandan Bora**	Pataal Bhairavi *(Novel)*	*1988*
♠ **Hiren Gohain**	Asomiya Jatiya Jibanot Mahapurushiya Parampara *(Literary Criticism)*	*1989*
♠ **Sneha Devi (Posthumously)**	Sneha Devir Ekunki Galpo *(Short Stories)*	*1990*
♠ **Ajit Baruah**	Brahmaputra Ityadi Padya *(Poetry)*	*1991*
♠ **Hiren Bhattacharya**	Saisar Pothar Manuh *(Poetry)*	*1992*
♠ **Keshav Mahanta**	Mor Je Kim an Henpah *(Poetry)*	*1993*
♠ **Silabhadra**	Madhupur Bahu Door *(Short Stories)*	*1994*
♠ **Chandraprasad Saikia**	Maharathi *(Novel)*	*1995*
♠ **Nirupama Borgohain**	Abhijatri *(Novel)*	*1996*
♠ **Nagen Saikia**	Aandharot Nijor Mukh *(Short Stories)*	*1997*

RECIPIENTS	PUBLICATIONS	YEAR
♦ **Arun Sarma**	Ashirbador Rang *(Novel)*	*1998*
♦ **Medini Choudhury**	Bipanna Samay *(Novel)*	*1999*
♦ **Apurba Sarma**	Baghe Tapur Rati *(Short Stories)*	*2000*
♦ **Mohim Bora**	Edhani Mahir Hanhi *(Novel)*	*2001*
♦ **Nalinidhar Bhattacharya**	Mahat Oitijya *(Criticism)*	*2002*
♦ **Bireswar Baruah**	Anek Manuh, Anek Thai Aaru Nirjanata *(Poetry)*	*2003*
♦ **Hirendra Nath Dutta**	Manuh Anukule *(Poetry)*	*2004*
♦ **Yeshe Dorze Thongchi**	Moun Ounth Mukhar Hriday *(Novel)*	*2005*
♦ **Atulananda Goswami**	Seneh Jurir Ganthi *(Short Story Collection)*	*2006*
♦ **Purabi Bormudoi**	Shantanu Kulanandan	*2007*
♦ **Rita Choudhury**	Deu Langkhui	*2008*
♦ **Dr Dhrubajyoti Bora**	Katha Ratnakar *(Novel)*	*2009*
♦ **Keshada Mahanta**	Assomiya Ramayani Sahitya : Kathabostur Atiguri *(Criticism)*	*2010*
♦ **Kabin Phukan (Posthumously)**	Aei anuragi aei udas (Poetry)	*2011*
♦ **Chandana Goswami**	Patkair Epare Mor Desh *(Novel)*	*2012*
♦ **Arupa Patangia Kalita**	Mariam Astin Athaba Hira Barua*(Short Stories)*	*2014*
♦ **Kula Saikia**	Akashar Chhabi Aru Anyanya Galpa *(Short Stories)*	*2015*
♦ **Jnan Pujari**	*Maghmalar Bhraman (Poetry)*	*2016*
♦ **Jayanta Modhab Bora**	*Moriahala (Novel)*	*2017*
♦ **Sananta Tanti** ♦ **Rituraj Basumatary** ♦ **Loknath Upadhyay Chapagain**	*Kailoir Dinto Amar Hobo (Poems)* *Dwngse Lama' (Short Story)* *Kino Royeu Upamaa (Short Story)*	*2018*

• **Asom Ratna Award:** Asom Ratna is the highest civilian award in the State of Assam. It is being conferred for outstanding contribution in literature, art and culture and social service. The award is offered by the Government of Assam.

Recipients

♦ Dr Bhupen Hazarika for the year 2009

♦ Mamoni Raisom Goswami (posthumously) for the year 2010

♦ Dr. Jitendra Nath Goswami for the year 2015

• Awards in the hallowed memory of legendary persons of Assam

Name of the Awards	Year of Introduction
• Srimanta Sankardeva Award	1986
• Ajan Peer Award	2004
• Fakhruddin Ali Ahmed Memorial Award	2005
• Siu-ka- Pha Award	2005
• Bir Chilarai Award	2006
• K. K. Handique Memorial Award	2006
• Madhabdeva Award	2009
• Kalicharan Brahma Award	2009
• Gopinath Bordoloi Award	
• Bishnu Rabha Award	1993
• Silpi Award	1999
• State Film Award	1999
• Natasurjya Phani Sarma Award	2004
• Amal Prabha Das Award	2006
• Chandra Prabha Saikiani Award	2006
• Sahityasarjya Atul Chandra Hazarika Award	2008
• Dr. Bhabendra Nath Saikia Award	2009
• Asom Ratna Award	2008
• Birendra Kumar Bhattacharjya Award	2009
• Ganesh Gogoi Award	2009
• Mamoni Roisom Award	2013
• Sati Sadhani Award	2015
• Ahmed Ali Baskandi Award	2015
• Syed Abdul Malik Award	2015
• Sonit Konwar Gajen Barua Award	2017

Gopinath Bardoloi Award (National Award) — 1993			
RECIPIENTS	YEAR	RECIPIENTS	YEAR
• Niketu Iralu	: —	• Shakuntala Choudhury	: —
Ajan Peer Award (National Award)			
RECIPIENTS	YEAR	RECIPIENTS	YEAR
• Rekibuddin Ahmed	: *2004*	• Dr. Birendra Nath Datta	: *2007*
• Hem Bhai	: *2005*	• Imran Shah	: *2008*

RECIPIENTS	YEAR	RECIPIENTS	YEAR
• Tafajjul Ali	: *2006*	• Arun Sarma	: *2015*
	Fakhruddin Ali Ahmed Award (National Award)		
RECIPIENTS	**YEAR**	**RECIPIENTS**	**YEAR**
• Sunil Dutta	: *2005*	• M. J. Akbar	: *2008*
• Shekhar Gupta	: *2006*	• Hema Bharali	: *2009*
• Shabana Azmi	: *2007*		
	Sui-ka-Pha Award (National Award)		
RECIPIENTS	**YEAR**	**RECIPIENTS**	**YEAR**
• Natwar Thakkar	: *2005*	• Rong Bong Terang	: *2009*
• Ratan Thiam	: *2006*	• Dr. Puspa Gogoi	: *2010*
• Padma Borkotoky	: *2007*	• Taburam Taid	: *2011*
• Dr. Jogendra Nath Phukan	: *2008*	• Khagendra Nath Saikia	: *2014*
	Bir Chilarai Award (National Award)		
RECIPIENTS	**YEAR**	**RECIPIENTS**	**YEAR**
• Sarat Ch. Singh	: *2006*	• Ambika Charan Choudhury	: *2008*
• Captain Jintu Gogoi	: *2007*		
	K. K. Handique Memorial Award (National Award)		
RECIPIENTS	**YEAR**	**RECIPIENTS**	**YEAR**
• Prof. Mukunda Madhab Sarma	: *2008*	• Dr. Jogendra Narayan Bhuyan	: *2010*
	Madhabdev Award (National Award)		
RECIPIENTS	**YEAR**	**RECIPIENTS**	**YEAR**
• Dr. Laxminandan Bora	: *2009*	• Prof. Mrinal Miri	: *2013*
	Kalicharan Brahma Award (National Award)		
RECIPIENTS	**YEAR**	**RECIPIENTS**	**YEAR**
• Dr. Pramod Ch. Bhattacharya	: *2009*	• Dr. Satyendra Narayan Goswami	: —
	Bishnu Rabha Award (State Award) — 1993		
RECIPIENTS	**YEAR**	**RECIPIENTS**	**YEAR**
• Pradip Chaliha and Gunada Das	: *1993*	• Nilapawan Baruah,	: *2005*
• Krishnamurti Hazarika, Nirmal Chakravarty and Khagen Das	: *1994*	• Hemangini Bardoloi, Benu Mishra,	: *2006*
• Girish Choudhury, Tafajjul Ali, Bibekananda Bhattacharya	: *1995*	• Gouri Barman, Indira P.P. Borah	: *2007*

RECIPIENTS	YEAR	RECIPIENTS	YEAR
• Sobha Brahma, Abdul Majid, Bina Das Manna	: *1996*	• Saranan Borthakur, Trailokya Dutta	: *2008*
• Mukunda Das Bhattacharya, Pratima Pande Baruah, Anupama Bhattacharya	: *1997*	• Nani Barpuzari, Dipali Das Bhuyan	: *2009*
• Mohan Lal Mukharjyee, Gopal Das	: *1998*	• Biren Singha, Ranjana Sarma Bardoloi	: *2010*
• Addya Sarma, Ajit Singha	: *1999*	• Santi Sankar Dasgupta, Durlabha Moran	: *2011*
• Makhan Prasad Duara, Kesab Mahanta, Pranab Baruah	: *2000*	• Ramesh Ghoush, Joya Saikia Duwarah	: *2012*
• Gakul Pathak, Sarbananda Medak	: *2001*	• Gorima Hazarika, Saleha Ahmed	: *2013*
• Medini Choudhury, Gyanada Kakoti	: *2002*	• Nalini Kanta Baruah, Hela Das, Aaimoni Gogoi	: *2014*
• Muhuni Rabha, Hemoram Nath, Ramen Baruah	: *2003*	• Krishna Das Nath, Rabi Ram Brahma	: *2015*
• Manoranjan Lahari, Braja Phukan	: *2004*	• Bipul Das, Girish Ch. Bora	: *2016*

Silpi Award (State Award) — 1999

RECIPIENTS	YEAR	RECIPIENTS	YEAR
• Pranab Das, Indreswar Pegu	: *1999*	• Minoti Khaound, Pranab Bora	: *2008*
• Dr. Bhabendra Nath Saikia, Jogen Chetia	: *2000*	• Mihir Bardoloi, Indreswar Sarma	: *2009*
• Dilip Sarma, Praphulla Bora, Prabhat Sarma	: *2001*	• Dipali Barthakur, Archana Mahanta	: *2010*
• Sudhakkhina Sarma, Mahendra Barthakur	: *2002*	• Jitu Sarma, Tapan Bhattacharya	: *2011*
• Soila Baruah, Dr. Lakhyahira Das	: *2003*	• Apurba Kr. Das, Dr. Dilip Ranjan Barthakur	: *2012*
• Bharat Barpuzari, Nikhilesh Baruah	: *2004*	• Jyotirmoy Kakoti, Hiren Gohain	: *2013*
• Bhaben Ray Patgiri, Bina Bhagawati	: *2005*	• Nurul Haque, Rajeswar Bardoloi	: *2014*
• Khagen Mahanta, Dilip Choudhury	: *2006*	• Kirti Kamal Bhuyan, Dipen Boruah	: *2015*
• Ganesh Pegu, Rameshwar Pathak	: *2007*	• Geeta Hatikakoti, Anupam Choudhury	: *2016*

Natasurya Phani Sarma Award (State Award) — 2004			
RECIPIENTS	**YEAR**	**RECIPIENTS**	**YEAR**
• **Tulshi Das**	: *2004*	• **Hasan Sarif Ahmed**	: *2011*
• **Ratna Oja**	: *2005*	• **Bishnu Khargharia**	: *2012*
• **Dharanidhar Choudhury**	: *2006*	• **Uday Sankar Saikia**	: *2013*
• **Gyanada Bora, Mahananda Sarma**	: *2007*	• **Nipon Goswami**	: *2014*
• **Bidya Rao Nayar**	: *2008*	• **Bholanath Kalita**	: *2015*
• **O.P. Nayar**	: *2009*	• **Bhola Kotoki**	: *2016*
• **Indra Bania**	: *2010*		
Chandra Prabha Saikiani Award (State Award) — 2006			
RECIPIENTS	**YEAR**	**RECIPIENTS**	**YEAR**
• **Charnaprabha Mahanta**	: *2008*	• **Minakshi Bhuyan**	: *2013*
• **Dr. Sukha Baruah**	: *2010*		
Amal Prabha Das (State Award) — 2006			
RECIPIENTS	**YEAR**	**RECIPIENTS**	**YEAR**
• **Mina Agarwala**	: *2008*	• **Miladoi Medok**	: *2013*
• **Eli Ahmed**	: *2010*		
Asom Ratna Award (State Award) — 2008			
RECIPIENTS	**YEAR**	**RECIPIENTS**	**YEAR**
• **Dr. Bhupen Hazarika**	: *2008*	• **Dr. Jitendra Nath Goswami**	: *2015*
• **Dr. Mamoni Roisom Goswami**	: *2012*		
Sahityacharjya Atul Ch., Hazarika Award (State Award) — 2008			
RECIPIENTS	**YEAR**	**RECIPIENTS**	**YEAR**
• **Achyut Lahkar**	: *2008*	• **Ratan Lahkar**	: *2010*
• **Hemanta Dutta**	: *2009*	• **Dharani Barman**	: *2015*
Dr. Bhabendra Nath Saikia Award (State Award)			
RECIPIENTS	**YEAR**	**RECIPIENTS**	**YEAR**
• **Jahnu Baruah**	: *2009*	• **Biju Phukan**	: *2010*
Birendra Bhattacharya Award (State Award) — 2009			
RECIPIENTS	**YEAR**	**RECIPIENTS**	**YEAR**
• **Radhika Mohan Bahagawati**	: *2009*		
Ganesh Gogoi Award (State Award) — 2009			
RECIPIENTS	**YEAR**	**RECIPIENTS**	**YEAR**
• **Hiren Bhattacharya**	: *2009*	• **Mahim Bora**	: *2015*
• **Ajit Baruah**	: *2010*		
Mamoni Roisom Goswami Award (State Award) — 2014			
RECIPIENTS	**YEAR**	**RECIPIENTS**	**YEAR**
• **Nirupama Bargohain**	: *2014*		

Sati Sadhani Award (State Award) — 2015			
RECIPIENTS	**YEAR**	**RECIPIENTS**	**YEAR**
• **Dr. Nomal Borah**	: *2015*		
Baskandi Sheikh Ahmed Ali Award (State Award) — 2015			
RECIPIENTS	**YEAR**	**RECIPIENTS**	**YEAR**
• **Moulana Taybur Rahman Barbhuyan**	: *2015*		
Syed Abdul Malik Award (State Award) — 2015			
RECIPIENTS	**YEAR**	**RECIPIENTS**	**YEAR**
• **Lt. Praphulla Ch. Borah**	: *2015*		
Sonit Konwar Gajen Barua Award — 2017			
RECIPIENTS	**YEAR**	**RECIPIENTS**	**YEAR**
• **Nrityasarjya Jatin Goswami**	: *2017*		

Museums under the Directorate of Museums

Dhubri District Museum:

Year of Establishment: 6th July, 1988

Location: District Library campus, Dhubri

Nilima Barua Folk Art Museum, Gauripur (a wing of Dhubri Museum)

Location : Bishnu Rabha Path, Gauripur, Dhubri

Barpeta District Museum, Barpeta

Year of Establishment : 1987

Location : Ward no1, Bilor tari hati, Barpeta

District Museum, Mangaldai

Year of Establishment : 1987

District Museum Tezpur

Year of Establishment : 1986

Location : Opp to D.C's office, Tezpur

District Museum, Nagaon

Year of Establishment : 1996

Gopinath Bordoloi Memorial Museum, Raha, Nagaon District

District Museum Jorhat:

Year of Establishment : 1996

Location : Opp. Irrigation Office, Siksha Bhawan Campus, Jorhat

Dibrugarh District Museum, Dibrugarh

Year of Establishment : 1996

Location : Milan Nagar CR Building, Maan Kota Road, Dibrugarh-3

Name	**Location**
• **Assam State Museum,**	Guwahati
• **Mayong Central Museum and Emporium**	Mayong
• **Srimanta Sankaradeva Kalakshetra**	Guwahati

17 Books and Authors

The literature of Assam is very rich and as such, the state of Assam is bestowed with several good books and many eminent writers. Below are mentioned the names of some of the popular books of Assam and their authors.

BOOKS	YEAR OF PUBLICATION	AUTHORS
Ahuti (Offerings)	*(1962)*	**Ambikagiri Raichoudhury**
Abhiyatri	*(1992)*	**Nirupama borgohain**
Adhunik Asomiya Sabdakosh	*(1991)*	**Sumanta Chaliha**
Aadhunik Asomiya Sahityor Buranji	*(1936)*	**Dimbeswar Neog**
Aai *(Mother)*	*(1960)*	**Dr Birendra Kumar Bhattacharya**
Akashbanti	*(1967)*	**Nilima Dutta**
Aghori Aatmaar Kahini *(A Tale of Nomadic Soul)*	*(1962)*	**Syed Abdul Malik**
Aahuti *(Offerings)*	*(1962)*	**Ambikagiri Raichoudhury**
Aadhunik Asomiya Biswakosh	*(1994)*	**Surjya Hazarika (Ed.)**
Alakaloi Chithi *(Letter to Alaka)*	*(1949)*	**Haliram Deka**
American Missionarysakal Aaru Unnabinsa Satikar Asom	*(1983)*	**Herambakanta Barpujari**
Arghayavali	*(1964)*	**Benudhar sharma**
Asomiya Aaru Engraji Abhidhan *(Anglo-Assamese Dictionary)*	*(1867)*	***Miles Bronson***
Asomiya Bhasha Aaru Sanskriti *(Assamese Language and Culture)*	*(1967)*	**Birinchi Kumar Baruah**
Asomiya Biswakosh *(Assamese Encyclopaedia)*	*(1980)*	**Kanak Chandra Mahanta**
Asomiya Sahityar Buranji	*(1957)*	**Debendranath Bezbaruah**
Asomiya Upanyasar Bhumika	*(1965)*	**Satyendranath Sarma**
Asomiya Vyakaran *(Assamese Grammar)*	*(1859)*	**Hemchandra Baruah**

📖	**Bahire Rang Chang Bhitare**	*(1876)*	✍	**Hemchandra Baruah**
📖	**Kowabhaturi** *(Playing in the Parlour, Empty in the Larder)*			
📖	**Banduka Behar**	*(1976)*	✍	**Medini Choudhaury**
📖	**Banphool** *(Wild Flowers)*	*(1952)*	✍	**Jatindranath Duarah**
📖	**Bedonar Ulka**	*(1964)*	✍	**Ambikagiri Raichoudhury**
📖	**Benudhar Sarma**	*(1983)*	✍	**Tirthanath Sarma**
📖	**Bharatar Swadhinata Sangramat Asomor Abadan**	*(1988)*	✍	**Laksminath Tamuli**
📖	**Bihugeet Aru Bonghosa**	*(1961)*	✍	**Lila Gogoi**
📖	**Bismrita Byatikram**	*(1981)*	✍	**Munin Borkotoki**
📖	**Choi Dasakor Gadya**	*(2002)*	✍	**Bhabendra Nath Saikia**

📖	**Cintanal** *(Burning Thoughts)*	*(1809)*	✍	**Kamalakanta Bhattacharya**
📖	**Cultural History of Assam, A**	*(1969)*	✍	**Birinchi Kumar Baruah**
📖	**Dasham**		✍	**Srimanta Sankardeva**
📖	**Deou Langkhui**	*(2005)*	✍	**Rita Choudhury**
📖	**Discovery of Assam**	*(1962)*	✍	**Satish Chandra Kakati**
📖	**Ejak Manuh, Ekhon Aranya**	*(1986)*	✍	**Umakanta Sarma**
📖	**Few Remarks on Assamese Language, A**	*(1849)*	✍	**Anandaram Dhekial Phukan**
📖	**Gita** *(Translation)*	*(1986)*	✍	**Mahendra Bora**
📖	**Gramatical Notes** *(Later Notes)* **of the Assamese Language**	*(1848)*	✍	**Nathan Brown**
📖	**Grammar of Assamese Language, A**	*(1839)*	✍	**W. Robinson**
📖	**Halodhiya Charaye Baodhan Khai**	*(1973)*	✍	**Homen Borgohain**
📖	**Hemkosh**	*(1900)*	✍	**Hemchandra Baruah**
📖	**History of Assamese Literature**	*(1964)*	✍	**Birinchi Kumar Baruah**
📖	**Jiban Britta** *(The Circle of Life)*	*(1999)*	✍	**Bhabendranath Saikia**
📖	**Jivan Rekha**	*(2002)*	✍	**Bhabendra Nath Saikia**
📖	**Kamini Kanta**	*(1877)*	✍	**G. S. Gurney**
📖	**Kirtan Ghosha** *(The Lyric in praise of God's Glory)*		✍	**Sankardeva**
📖	**Lohitya-Sindhu**	*(1997)*	✍	**Tilottama Mishra**
📖	**Loka Kalpadristi**	*(1987)*	✍	**Nilamoni Phukan**

🕮 **Mahatmar Pora Rupkonwaraloi**	*(1969)*	✍ **Lakshminath Phukan**
🕮 **Maniram Dewan**	*(1996)*	✍ **Benudhar Sarma**
🕮 **Miri Jiyori**	*(1894)*	✍ **Rajanikanta Bordoloi**
🕮 **Mor Jiban Suwaran**	*(1944)*	✍ **Lakshminath Bezbaruah**
🕮 **Mor Sambadik Jiban** *(My Journalist Life)*	*(1989)*	✍ **Homen Borgohain**
🕮 **Mrityunjoy**	*(1970)*	✍ **Birendra Kr. Bhattacharya**
🕮 **Nama-Ghosha**		✍ **Madhabdeva**
🕮 **Neelakanthi Brajo**	*(1976)*	✍ **Mamoni Raisom Goswami**
🕮 **New Light on History of Assamese Literature**	*(1962)*	✍ **Dimbeswar Neog**
🕮 **Omar Tirtha** *(Translation)*	*(1925)*	✍ **Jatindranath Duarah**
🕮 **Pabitra Asom**	*(1960)*	✍ **Maheswar Neog**
🕮 **Pataal-Bhairavi**	*(1968)*	✍ **Lakshminandan Bora**
🕮 **Pita-Putra**	*(1975)*	✍ **Homen Borgohain**
🕮 **Rajpathe Ringiyaye** *(The Call of the Highway)*	*(1955)*	✍ **Birendra Kumar Bhattacharya**
🕮 **Rupalim**	*(1960)*	✍ **Jyoti Prasad Agarwalla**
🕮 **Ruptirthar Yatri**	*(1965)*	✍ **Sayed Abdul Malik**

🕮 **Cintanal** *(Burning Thoughts)*	*(1809)*	✍ **Kamalakanta Bhattacharya**
🕮 **Cultural History of Assam, A**	*(1969)*	✍ **Birinchi Kumar Baruah**
🕮 **Dasham**		✍ **Srimanta Sankardeva**
🕮 **Deou Langkhui**	*(2005)*	✍ **Rita Choudhury**
🕮 **Discovery of Assam**	*(1962)*	✍ **Satish Chandra Kakati**
🕮 **Ejak Manuh, Ekhon Aranya**	*(1986)*	✍ **Umakanta Sarma**
🕮 **Few Remarks on Assamese Language, A**	*(1849)*	✍ **Anandaram Dhekial Phukan**
🕮 **Gita** *(Translation)*	*(1986)*	✍ **Mahendra Bora**
🕮 **Gramatical Notes** *(Later Notes)* **of the Assamese Language**	*(1848)*	✍ **Nathan Brown**
🕮 **Grammar of Assamese Language, A**	*(1839)*	✍ **W. Robinson**
🕮 **Halodhiya Charaye Baodhan Khai**	*(1973)*	✍ **Homen Borgohain**
🕮 **Hemkosh**	*(1900)*	✍ **Hemchandra Baruah**
🕮 **History of Assamese Literature**	*(1964)*	✍ **Birinchi Kumar Baruah**
🕮 **Jiban Britta** *(The Circle of Life)*	*(1999)*	✍ **Bhabendranath Saikia**

🕮 **Jivan Rekha**	*(2002)*	✍ **Bhabendra Nath Saikia**
🕮 **Kamini Kanta**	*(1877)*	✍ **G. S. Gurney**
🕮 **Kirtan Ghosha** *(The Lyric in praise of God's Glory)*		✍ **Sankardeva**
🕮 **Lohitya-Sindhu**	*(1997)*	✍ **Tilottama Mishra**
🕮 **Loka Kalpadristi**	*(1987)*	✍ **Nilamoni Phukan**
🕮 **Mahatmar Pora Rupkonwaraloi**	*(1969)*	✍ **Lakshminath Phukan**
🕮 **Maniram Dewan**	*(1996)*	✍ **Benudhar Sarma**
🕮 **Miri Jiyori**	*(1894)*	✍ **Rajanikanta Bordoloi**
🕮 **Mor Jiban Suwaran**	*(1944)*	✍ **Lakshminath Bezbaruah**
🕮 **Mor Sambadik Jiban** *(My Journalist Life)*	*(1989)*	✍ **Homen Borgohain**
🕮 **Mrityunjoy**	*(1970)*	✍ **Birendra Kr. Bhattacharya**
🕮 **Nama-Ghosha**		✍ **Madhabdeva**
🕮 **Neelakanthi Brajo**	*(1976)*	✍ **Mamoni Raisom Goswami**
🕮 **New Light on History of Assamese Literature**	*(1962)*	✍ **Dimbeswar Neog**
🕮 **Omar Tirtha** *(Translation)*	*(1925)*	✍ **Jatindranath Duarah**
🕮 **Pabitra Asom**	*(1960)*	✍ **Maheswar Neog**
🕮 **Pataal-Bhairavi**	*(1968)*	✍ **Lakshminandan Bora**
🕮 **Pita-Putra**	*(1975)*	✍ **Homen Borgohain**
🕮 **Rajpathe Ringiyaye** *(The Call of the Highway)*	*(1955)*	✍ **Birendra Kumar Bhattacharya**
🕮 **Rupalim**	*(1960)*	✍ **Jyoti Prasad Agarwalla**
🕮 **Ruptirthar Yatri**	*(1965)*	✍ **Sayed Abdul Malik**
🕮 **Sandhyar Sur (The Music of Sunset)**	*(1928)*	✍ **Nalinibala Devi**
🕮 **Yaruyingam**	*(1960)*	✍ **Birendra Kumar Bhattacharya**
🕮 **Sri Sri Sankardeva**	*(1948)*	✍ **Maheswar Neog**
🕮 **Uttarakanda Ramayana**		✍ **Srimanta Sankardeva**
🕮 **Vinsho Shatabdir Asomiya Sahitya**	*(1967)*	✍ **Homen Borgohain (Ed.)**
🕮 **Sankhipta Asomiya Biswakosh** *(Concise Assamese Encylopedia)*	*(2001)*	✍ **Santanu Kaushik Baruah**
🕮 **Soingya Abhiddhan**	*(2010)*	✍ **Santanu Kausik Baruah**

Some Religious Books of Assam	
Books	**Authors**
🕮 **Anadi Patan**	✍ Srimanta Sankardeva
🕮 **Bhakti Ratnakar**	✍ Srimanta Sankardeva
🕮 **Bhakti Pradip**	✍ Srimanta Sankardeva
🕮 **Bhakti Gunamala**	✍ Srimanta Sankardeva
🕮 **Dasham**	✍ Srimanta Sankardeva
🕮 **Kirtan Ghosha**	✍ Srimanta Sankardeva
🕮 **Nimi Navasidha Sam bad**	✍ Srimanta Sankardeva
🕮 **Nama Ghosha**	✍ Madhabdeva
🕮 **Srimad Bhagavad Gita**	✍ Translated by - Bhattadeva

18 Sports and Games

Assam has come a long way in regard to sports and games with the spirit of sports deeply ingrained in the people of Assam. Assam has emerged as a major sports power in India. It has given many dynamic sports personalities to the nation , as well as to the world who have made Assam proud and whose performances speak volumes about the ability of the Assamese sportspersons. Some famous names in this context include Bhogeshwar Baruah, Monalisha Baruah Mehta (Table Tennis Player), Talimeron Ao (Football Player), Shiva Thapa (Boxer) Gilbertson Sangma (Footballer), Tashen Bora, Dipankar Bhattacharya (Badminton Player), Babul Phukan, Pradip Brahma, Mithu Baruah, Jayanta Talukdar (Archery), Abu Nachim, Fariha Zaman, etc.

Bordoloi Trophy

The Bordoloi Trophy is the biggest soccer rather sporting event of Assam and of the North East India as a whole. Titled after Bharat Ratna - Lokapriya Gopinath Bordoloi, this trophy was organized by the Guwahati Town Club for the exposure of the football players of this region in the national and the international arena.

List of Bordoloi Trophy winners :

Year	Winners	Runners Up
1952	*Railway Sports Club, Pandu*	Union Sporting Club (Nowgong)
1953	*Maharana AC, Guwahati*	Shillong Garrison
1954	*Guwahati Town Club*	Silchar India Club
1955	*State Transport Association, Shillong*	Thangalbari Club. Jorhat
1956	*Guwahati Town Club and State Transport Association, Shillong (Joint holders)*	—
1957	*Jalpaiguri TC, West Bengal*	Guwahati Town Club
1958	*Southern Railway Institute, Mysore*	Maharana AC, Guwahati
1959	*Sporting Union Club, Guwahati*	City College Old Boys FC, Hyderabad
1960	*Dergaon Police AC, Oergaon*	Assam Rifles
1961	*Mysore District, Mysore*	Assam Rifles
1962	*Leader Football Club, Jallandhar*	Howrah Union, Calcutta
1963	*Leader Football Club, Jallandhar and Guwahati Town Club (Joint holders)*	—
1964	*Assam Rifles, Agartala*	Jalpaiguri TC, W. Bengal

Year	Winners	Runners Up
1965	*Aryan Club, Calcutta*	Md. Sporting, Calcutta
1966	*Aryan Club, Calcutta*	Md. Sporting, Calcutta
1967	*Eastern Railway, Calcutta*	Ichapur Rifle Factory
1968	*East Bengal, Calcutta*	Eastern Railway, Calcutta
1969	*Md. Sporting, Calcutta*	East Bengal, Calcutta
1970	*Md. Sporting, Calcutta*	Khidirpur Club, Calcutta
1971	*Assam Police, Assam*	Md. Sporting, Calcutta
1972	*East Bengal, Calcutta*	Dacca-XI, Bangladesh
1973	*East Bengal, Calcutta*	Leader Football, Jalandhar
1974	*Mohun Bagan, Calcutta*	Vasco SC, Goa
1975	*Mohun Bagan, Calcutta*	Punjab-XI
1976	*Mohun Bagan, Calcutta*	Goa-XI
1977	*Mohun Bagan, Calcutta*	Md. Sporting, Calcutta
1978	*East Bengal, Calcutta*	Port Authority, Bangkok
1979	*Port Authority, Bangkok*	Oil India, Duliajan, Assam
1980	***Not held***	—
1981	*Assam Police, Assam*	Dempo SC, Goa
1982	*Dempo SC, Goa*	Md. Sporting, Calcutta
1983	*Md. Sporting, Calcutta*	Assam Police, Assam
1984	*Mohun Bagan, Calcutta*	Mafatlal SC, Bombay
1985	*Md. Sporting, Calcutta*	Salgaoncar Club, Goa
1986	*Md. Sporting, Calcutta*	PSEB, Punjab
1987	*Khidirpur SC, Calcutta*	Assam Rifles
1988	*ASEB Sports Club, Guwahati*	Assam Rifles
1989	*Isteghlal Club, Iran*	Dhaka Md. Sporting
1990	*Oil India-XI, Duliajan*	Shillong-XI
1991	*Md. Sporting, Calcutta*	East Bengal, Calcutta
1992	*East Bengal, Calcutta*	BSF, Jallandhar
1993	*Port Authority FC, Bangkok*	Mohun Bagan, Calcutta
1994	*Punjab Police, Punjab*	Mizoram-XI
1995	*Assam Police, Assam Academy*	Williamson Magar Football
1996	*Mohun Bagan, Calcutta*	East Bengal, Calcutta ,
1997	*Assam Police, Assam*	Aizawi-XI
1998	*Navabakhar Club, Uzbekistan*	TRAV, lmphal
1999	*Assam Regimental Centre, Shillong*	ASEB SC, Guwahati
2000	*Tata Football Academy, Jamshedpur*	ASRF, Diphu, Assam.
2001	*Mohun Bagan, Calcutta*	Rajpracha Football Club, Bangkok
2002	*Assam Regimental Centre*	Assam State Electricity Board
2003	*Regimental Centre, Shillong*	Oil India, Assam
2004	*Brothers Union, Bangladesh*	Shillong - XI

Year	Winners	Runners Up
2005	*Assam Regimental Centre, Shillong*	SAIL, Kolkata
2006	*Assam State Electricity Board*	Assam Regimental Centre. Shillong
2007	*Port Authority, Bangkok*	ONGC, Mumbai
2008	*Oil India Football Club (Duliajan)*	ASEB
2009	*ASEB*	Nagaland Police
2010	*Abahoni Limited (Dhaka)*	Three Star Club (Nepal)
2011	*Royal Wahingdoh F.C., Shillong*	Langsning SC, Shillong
2012	*Oil India Limited (Duliajan)*	Assam Rifles
2013	*Bhawanipore F.C.*	Aizawl FC
2014	*Assam State Electricity Board*	Green Valley F.C.
2015	***Not held***	—
2016	*Three Star Club*	East Bengal
2018	*Mohammedan Sporting Club*	Oil India

Apart from the Bordoloi Trophy, there are many other trophies and cups which hold their own importance. These trophies include the Independence Cup (Football), ATPA Shield (Football), Dugar Shield (Football), Mahendra Mohan Choudhury Trophy (Football), Uttam Barman Gold Cup (Football) Upen Brahma Gold Cup (Football), etc.

Stadiums In Assam

Indira Gandhi Stadium and Nehru Stadium are the important stadiums in Assam. The other stadiums located in Assam are:

Stadium		Place
Indira Gandhi Athletic Stadium	:	Guwahati
Jawaharlal Nehru Stadium	:	Guwahati
Jorhat Stadium	:	Jorhat
Assam Cricket Association Stadium	:	Guwahati
Nurul Amin Stadium	:	Nagoan
Satindra Mohan Dev Stadium	:	Silchar
Karmabir Nabin Chandra Bordoloi AC Indoor Hall	:	Sarusajai
Dr. Zakir Hussain Aquatic Complex	:	Sarusajai
Maulana MD Tayabullah Hockey Stadium	:	Guwahati
North East Frontier Railway Stadium	:	Guwahati

Adventure Sports : Assam is heaven for those who loves adventure sports. The land is full of wildlife, caves, mountain, rivers etc. Which make it perfect place to do adventure sports. Adventure lovers can enjoy mountaineering, trekking, para-sailing, hang-gliding, river crossing, river rafting, angling, etc.

19 Press

Language : Assamese (Asamiya) is the major language spoken by the people of Assam. It is a very rich language and has its origins in the ancient Sanskrit.

In addition to Assamese, the other recognized Indian languages spoken in the state include-

English, Hindi and Bengali. However, other indigenous languages like the Bodo, Karbi, Mishing, Rabha, Deuri, Nepali, etc. are also spoken in Assam.

Print Media : The history of Assamese print media is more than 168 years old. The journey was started with **Arunodoi**. It was first published in January,1846 from Sibsagar, Dr Nathan Brown was the first editor of the monthly magazine.

First In Magazines And Newspapers

First Newspaper	Arunodoi (Sunrise) 1846-1882, Editor : Dr Nahan Brown.
First English Daily	The Assam Tribune, its first editor was Lakshminath Phookan
First daily newspaper	Danik Batori (1835-1836) Editor : Nilamoni Phukan.
First weekly newspaper	Assam Mihir (1872-1873, Editor : Chidananda Choudhary (Das)
The oldest weekly newspaper still in circulation	Saptahik Janambhumi (1947), First Editor : Dulal Chandra Bhuyan
First newspaper published by a native	Assam Bilashini (1871-1830)
The first newspaper published with a political outlook	Advocate of Assam (1903-1910), Editor : Muthuramohan Barua
First Assamese satire magazine	Cartoon, Editor : Pulak Gogoi
First Assamese children magazine	Lora Bandhu (1888) Editor : Karunabhiram Barua
First Assamese woman magazine	Ghar Jeuty (1927 Editor : Kamalaya Kakoti
First school magazine	Prabhat (Jorhat Normal School, 1915), Editor : Saratchandra Goswami

First bi-lingual weekly	Assam News (1882-1885), Editor : Hemchandra Barua.
First bi-weekly newspaper	Asom Batori
First Assamese mini magazine	Bindu (1970), Editor : Bhupen Hazarika
First Assamese magazine published outside Assam	Jonaki (Moonlight)
The first special newspaper published exclusively for women	Uruli, Editor : Nalinibala Devi.
First magazine based on agricultural matters	Assam Krishak
First Assamese weekly magazine	Navajug (1963), Editor : Birendra Kumar Bhattacharya

Current Newspapers And News Channels In Assam

Assamese Dailies	Dainik Asom, Amar Asom, Dainik Agradoot, Asomiya Pratidin, Asomiya Khabar, Niyamiya Barta.
English Dailies	The Assam Tribune, The Sentinel, The North East Times, The Telegraph (Guwahati edition), Economic Daily.
Hindi Dailies	Purbanchal Prahari, Hindi Sentinel, Dainik Purbodaya, Khabar
Bengali Dailies	Sangbad Lahiri, Dainik Yugashankha, Dainik Sonar Cachar, Dainik Prantajyoti, Dainik Gati
Assamese weeklies	Asom Bani, Sadin, Agradoot (biweekly), Dalit Asom, Saptahik Alok, Janambhumi, Asom Spandan, Batabaran, Deshar Pragati, Amar Agniban, Kandari, Saptabarta, Purbanchal Batori,Paharidoot, Sapatahik Chetona, Kopili, Natun Batori, Ajir Gana Barud, Pabitra Asom, Saptahik Morigaon, Jamyat, Kabach, Mouchak, Saptahik Asomiya, Agnigarh, Mangol Batori, Sadiniya Bartaman, Louit Jyoti, Chetna.
English Weeklies	North East Echo, Challenger Barta, The Cachar Tribune, The Hills Times
Hindi Weekly	Akela, Newsline
Bengali Weeklies	Samayik Prasanga, Jugaskhakti, Nabayug, Dristipath, Tirthabhumi, Kushiara, Ananda Jyoti, Ghar Ghar, Karimganj Sambad, The Dibakar, The Purbayan, The Anirban Shikha, The Dalim, Arunoday, Gana Andolon.
Nepali Weekly	Deshbarta
Thado-Kuki Weekly	Voice of Songpijang
Bodo Weekly	Bodosa
Current New Channels in Assam	Dy 365, Focus NE, News Live, DD Northeast, Frontier TV, Prime News, News Time, Prag News, Khobor 365 Din.

20 Abbreviations

A

- **AAIDCL** : Assam Agro-Industries Development Corporation Limited.
- **AASU** : All Assam Student's Union.
- **ABILAC** : Anundoram Baruah Institute of Language, Art & Culture.
- **ABSU** : All Bodo Student's Union.
- **ACS** : Assam Civil Service.
- **AFC** : Assam Financial Corporation; Assam Fertilizer Corporation.
- **AFL** : Assam Fertichem Limited.
- **AGP** : Asom Gana Parishad.
- **AHSEC** : Assam Higher Secondary Education Council.
- **AIDC** : Assam Industrial Development Corporation.
- **AMC** : Assam Medical College.
- **APL** : Assam Petrochemicals Limited.
- **APOL** : Assam Polyester Co-operative Limited.
- **APSC** : Assam Public Service Commission.
- **ARIASP** : Assam Rural Infrastructure and Agricultural Services Project.
- **ASCARD**: Assam State Co-operative Agriculture and Rural Development Bank.
- **ASEB** : Assam State Electricity Board.
- **ASIDC** : Assam Small Industries Development Corporation Limited.
- **ASTC** : Assam State Transport Corporation.
- **ATC** : Assam Tea Corporation.
- **ATDC** : Assam Tourism Development Corporation.
- **AXX** : Asom Xahitya Xabha.

B

- **BAC** : Bodoland Autonomous Council.
- **BRPL** : Bongaigaon Refinery and Petrochemicals Limited.
- **BSS** : Bodo Sahitya Sabha.
- **BTC** : Bodoland Territorial Council.

D

- **DRDA** : District Rural Development Agency.

G

- **GMC** : Guwahati Municipal Corporation.
- **GMCH** : Gauhati Medical College and Hospital.
- **GU** : Gauhati University.

I

- **IITG** : Indian Institute of Technology, Guwahati.

J

- **JEC** : Jorhat Engineering College.
- **JRY** : Jawahar Rozgar Yojana.

N

- **NEC** : North-Eastern Council.
- **NEFA** : North-Eastern Frontier Agency.
- **NFR** : North-East Frontier Railway.
- **NIT** : National Institute of Technology.

S

- **SEBA** : Board of Secondary Education, Assam.
- **STATFED** : Assam State Co-operative, Marketing and Consumer's Federation Limited.

T

- **TRYSEM**: Training of Rural Youth For Self-Employment.

21 Miscellaneous

Biggest, Longest, Tallest Smallest of Assam

➲Biggest

Airport	:	Lokopriya Gopinath Bordoloi Airport(Borjhar)
City	:	Guwahati
Railway Station	:	Guwahati Railway Station
River	:	Brahmaputra (2900 km.)

➲Longest

River Bridge	:	Dhola-Sadiya Bridge (River-Brahmaputra)

➲Tallest

Temple	:	Shiva Dol

➲Smallest

District	:	Hailakandi
Inhabited River Island	:	Umananda

➲Largest

Museum	:	Assam State Museum
National Park	:	Manas National Park (500 sq. km.)
River Island	:	Majuli
Zoo	:	Assam State Zoo

➲Highest

Peak	:	Namcha Barwa (7782 m.)

➲Oldest

Buranji (History)	:	Puroni Asom Buranji
Modern Refinery	:	Digboi
Primitive Refinery	:	Margherita

- **Popularly Known As .....**

Person		Known As
• **Ananda Chandra Agarwalla**	:	Bhangoni Konwar
• **Ananda Chandra Baruah**	:	Bokulbonor Kavi
• **Anandiram Oas**	:	Bon Konwar
• **Ambeshwar Chetiya Phukan**	:	Kabita Konwar
• **Ambikagiri Rai Choudhury**	:	Asom Kesari

• **Birendra Kumar Phukan**	:	Sangeet Jyoti
• **Brajnath Sharma**	:	Abhinyacharya
• **Bhuwan Gogoi (Footballer)**	:	Assam Rhino
• **Benudhar Sharma**	:	Buronjibid
• **Binanda Chandra Baruah**	:	Dhwani Kavi
• **Bishnu Prasad Rabha**	:	Kalaguru
• **Bishnuram Medhi**	:	Lauha Manav
• **Chandra Kumar Agarwalla**	:	Protimaar Khonikar
• **Chandradhar Baruah**	:	Sahityaratna
• **Durgeshwar Sharma**	:	Daarshanik Kavi
• **Debeshwar Sharma**	:	Jananayak
• **Dharmeshwari Devi Baruwani**	:	Kaabya Bharati
• **Dr Upendra Kakati**	:	Ganashilpi
• **Dr Bhupen Hazarika**	:	Sangeet Surya, Sangeet Samrat
• **Dr Bhubaneshwar Baruah**	:	Lokabandhu
• **Gopinath Bordoloi**	:	Lokopriya
• **Ganesh Chandra Gogoi**	:	Paaporir Kavi
• **Gajen Baruah**	:	Sonit Konwar
• **Hem Baruah**	:	Assam Gaurav
• **Hiren Bhattacharya**	:	Sugandhi Pokhilaar Kavi
• **Hemchandra Baruah**	:	Tyaagveer
• **Jatindranath Duarah**	:	Banphoolor Kavi
• **Jyoti Prasad Agarwalla**	:	Rupkonwar
• **Kamalakanta Bhattacharya**	:	Agni Kavi
• **Kamala Nath (Footballer)**	:	Assam Mail
• **Krishnakant Handique**	:	Praachyo Pandit
• **Kanaklata Baruah**	:	Birbala
• **Lakshmidhar Sarm**	:	Deshpran
• **Lakshminath Bezbaruah**	:	Sahityarathi, Rasharaj
• **Mafijuddin Ahmed Hazarika**	:	Gyanmalinir Kavi
• **Motiram Bora**	:	Lokapran
• **Nalinibala Devi**	:	Atindriyabadi Kavi
• **Nilamoni Phukan**	:	Bagmibor
• **Nabin Chandra Bordoloi**	:	Karmaveer
• **Nirmalprabha Bordoloi**	:	Saraswati
• **Omiyo Kumar Das**	:	Lokanayak
• **Prasanlal Choudpury**	:	Biplavi Kavi
• **Padmanath Gohain Baruah**	:	Dronacharya
• **Parbati Prasad Baruah**	:	Geeti Kavi
• **Paragdhar Chaliha**	:	Seuj Konwar
• **Phani Sharma**	:	Natsurjya
• **Raghunath Choudhury**	:	Bihogi Kavi
• **Ratnakanta Barkakati**	:	Sewalir Kavi

• **Ram Gogoi**	:	Potharor Kavi
• **Rudra Baruah**	:	Luit Konwar
• **Radha Govinda Baruah**	:	Singha Purush
• **Rajanikanta Bordoloi**	:	Upanyas Samrat
• **Subir Choudhury (Footballer)**	:	Chinese Wall
• **Satya Prasad Baruah**	:	Natya Prabhakar
• **Sailadhar Rajkhowa**	:	Nijorar Kavi
• **Syed Abdul Malik**	:	Katha Silpi
• **Tarunram Phukan**	:	Deshbhakta

Major Historical Monuments of the State

Name of the Monument	Nearest Town	Period
Aswaklanta Mandir	Gurwahati	1725 AD
Bar Dol	Bishwanath	1750 Century AD
Basudev Dol	Gohpur	18th Century AD
Bezor Dol	Dibrugarh	18th Century AD
Billeswar Mandir	Nalbari	1521 AD
Gaurisagar Dol	Sibsagar	1724 AD
Gupteswar Mandir	Dhekiajuli	12th Century AD
Hayagriya Mandir	Hajo	1583 AD
Joi-Dol	Sibsagar	1698AD
Kareng Ghar	Nazira	17-18th Century AD
Kamakhya Mandir	Guwahati	1565 AD
Khaspur	Silchar	18th Century AD
Maghnowa Dol	Naranyanpur	17th Century AD
Maibang Mandir	Maibang	1761 AD
Negheriting Dol	Dibrugarh	18th Century AD
Panbari Masjid	Gauripuria	18th - 19th Century AD
Piyali Phukanar Dol	Nazira	19th Century AD
Raidongia Dol	Dibrugarh	18th Century AD
Rang Ghar	Sibsagar	18th Century AD
Rudrasagar Dol	Sibsagar	1698 AD
Shiva Dol	Sibsagar	1734 AD
Sonai Mandir	Silchar	1885 - 1887 AD
Thaora Dol	Sibsagar	1663-1685 AD

22 Important Events

Some Important Years and Events of Assam

YEARS	EVENTS
350	• Pushya Varman founded the Varman dynasty in Lower Assam.
594	• Bhaskar Varman, the best ruler of the Varman dynasty, who is also known as 'Kumar Raja', ascended the throne of Kamrup.
629	• Noted Chinese traveller Hiuen-Tsang visited Assam.
650	• Salastambha founded the Salastambha dynasty in Kamrup.
725	• Harshadeva, the most powerful king of the Salastambha dynasty, ascended the throne of Kamrup.
990	• Brahma Pala established Pala Dynasty in Kamarupa.
1100	• End of Pala Dynasty with the fell of last king Jaya Pala.
1206	• First Muslim invasion on Kamarupa.
1227	• Second Muslim invasion on Kamarupa.
1228	• Sukapha founded the Ahom Dynasty in Assam.
1253	• First capital of the Ahoms established at Charaideo.
1257	• Third Muslim invasion on Kamarupa.
1449	• Mahapurush Srimanta Sankardeva was born.
1490	• First Ahom-Kachari battle.
1498	• Alauddin Hussain Shah of Gaur attacked Nilambar, the king of Kamata, and occupied it.
1536	• Ahoms destroyed Dimapur, the capital of the Kachari kingdom.
1537	• Sankardeva migrated to the Koch kingdom.
1539	• Gargaon became the Ahom capital.
1539	• Suhungmung met his death as a result of a conspiracy hatched by his eldest son Suklenmung.
1548	• An earthquake of high intensity occurred.
1563	• Chilarai occupied Ahom capital Garhgaon, ended with Treaty of Majuli.
1568	• Srimanta Sankardev died.
1615	• First battle fought against the Mughals by the Ahoms under Pratap Singha.
1662	• Mirjumlah attacked Assam. Mirjumlah occupied Gargaon and Raja's Palace.
1671	• Ahom won Battle of Saraighat and Ram singh I retreated to Rangamati.
1681	• Last battle fought between the Ahoms and the Mughals at Itakhuli.
1694	• Umananda temple was built.
1769	• First phase of moamoria rebellion, Ahom Capital fell but recaptured in 1770.

1782 • Ahom capital Rangpur fell the second time to Moamoria rebellion. Rebel leaders striked coins in their names.

1794 • Ahom capital shifted to Jorhat from Rangpur.

1815 • The first Burmese invasion.

1819 • The second Burmese invasion.

1821 • The third Burmese invasion.

1823 • Tea was discovered in Assam.

1826 • Treaty of Yandaboo signed between the British and the Burmese.

1834 • First High school, established at Guwahati.

1837 • Bengali was introduced as a medium of instruction instead of Assamese.

1843 • First American Baptist Missionary started in Assam.

1846 • First journal-of Assam, ***'Orunodoi'***, published on 1st January.

1857 • Sepoy Mutiny.

1864 • The capital of Assam shifted from Cherrapunji to Shillong.

1865 • Telephone and Telegraph services introduced in Assam.

1871 • The first Assamese newspaper '***Assam Bilasini***' published in Assam.

1873 • Assamese instated as a medium of instruction.

1874 • Assam separated from Bengal.

1883 • Shipping services started on the mighty Brahmaputra.

1885 • Rail services started in Assam.

1886 • Myadi Settlement System introduced.

1888 • 'Asomiya Bhashar Unnoti Sadhini Sabha' formed at Calcutta on 25th August.

1889 • First Assamese monthly magazine, '***Jonaki***' was published from Calcutta on 9th January.

1889 • Crude oil was discovered in Assam.

1897 • Deadly earthquake casted 1542 lives (12th June).

1900 • The first and the biggest tea research centre of the world, the 'Tocklai Tea Research Centre' was established at Tocklai in Jorhat.

1901 • ***Cotton College***, named after 'Sir Henry Cotton', was established at Guwahati on 26th May.

• ***World's oldest oil refinery*** at Digboi started functioning.

1905 • Assam Association formed.

1916 • Assam Chatra Sanmilani formed.

1917 • First convention of Asom Sahitya Sabha took place on 26th December.

1920 • Non-cooperation movement began in Assam.

1921 • Mahatma Gandhi visited Assam.

1926 • 41st session of Congress was held at Pandu.

1935 • Autonomous rule introduced.

1937 • Ministry of Saadulla formed on April,1.

1940 • Assam State Museum established on 21st April at Guwahati.

1942 • Quit India Movement started.

• Kanaklata attained martyrdom.

1943 • Kushal Konwar hanged.

1947 • Assam got independence along with India.

• Gopinath Bordoloi became the first Chief Minister and Sir Akbar Hydari became the Governor of independent Assam.

1948 • First University of Assam, the Gauhati University, was established on 1st January.

1948 • All India Radio Centre, established at Guwahati on 1st July.

1948 • Gauhati High Court established.

1950 • Devastating earthquake rocked Assam on 15th August.

1955 • Jatindranath Duarah became the first Assamese to be honoured with the coveted 'Sahitya Akademi Award' for his masterpiece, 'Banphool'.

1955 • Krishnakanta Handique was honoured with the prestigious 'Padma Shri Award'.

1958 • Nalinibala Devi was honoured with 'Padma Shri Award'.

1959 • Regional Research Laboratory (RRL) established at Jorhat, on 18th March.

1960 • Language revolution took place.

• Panchayat formed.

1961 • Assamese gained recognition as State language.

1962 • Guwahati refinery established at Noonmati in Guwahati.

• Chinese invasion.

1965 • Dibrugarh University established at Dibrugarh.

1966 • Ambikagiri Raichoudhury was awarded with the 'Sahitya Akademi Award' for his *anthology, 'Bedonar Ulka'.*

1967 • Krishnakanta Handique honoured with the coveted 'Padma Bhushan Award'.

• Nalinibala Devi was honoured with the 'Sahitya Akademi Award' for her *masterpiece, 'Aiakananda'.*

1969 • Assam Agriculture University established at Jorhat.

• Atul Chandra Hazarika won the 'Sahitya Akademi Award' for his work, 'Manchalekha'.

1970 • Guwahati Tea Auction Centre established at Guwahati on 25th September.

1971 • Atul Chandra Hazarika honoured with the coveted 'Padmashri Award'.

1973 • 'Padmashri' conferred on Ananda Chandra Baruah.

1974 • The capital of Assam shifted from Shillong to Dispur (Guwahati).

1975 • Navakanta Baruah was awarded with the 'Sahitya Akademi Award' for his novel, 'Kokadeutar Har'.

1978 • Janata Dal ministry formed in Assam on 12th March.

• Sahitya Akademi Award conferred on Homen Borgohain for his book, 'Pita-Putra.'

1979 • Assam Agitation began on 8th June.

1979 • President's rule imposed in Assam for the first time on 12th December.

1985 • Assam Accord signed on 15th August.

• A regional party from Assam, A.G.P. (Asom Gana Parishad) took over the charge of governance for the first time on 24th December.

1987
- Kalia Bhomora Bridge, the second bridge over the mighty Brahmaputra, inaugurated at Tezpur on 14th April.
- First Lok Adalat opened at Hajo on 12th December.

1990
- President's rule imposed in Assam (27th November).

1991
- Congress ministry formed under the leadership of Hiteswar Saikia on 30th June.

1992
- Dr Bhupen Hazarika became the first Assamese to be awarded with the 'Dada Saheb Phalke Award'.

1993
- Noted literary personality, Navakanta Baruah, awarded with the coveted 'Assam Valley Literary Award'.

1994
- The first planetarium in the North-East the Guwahati Planetarium, established at Guwahati on 17th August.

1995
- 'Sahitya Akademi Award', conferred on Chandraprasad Saikia for his work 'Maharathi'.

1997
- Foundation stone laid for the fourth bridge over the mighty Brahmaputra at Bogibeel near Dibrugarh.
- 'Jnanpith Award' winner, Birendra Kumar Bhattacharya, passed away on 6th August.
- 'Assam Valley Literary Award', conferred on renowned poet, Nilamoni Phukan on 31st December.

1998
- 'Adajya', an Assamese movie, grabbed the special jury award in the Asian Film Director's category at the 'International Film Festival' on 20th January.
- 'Srimanta Sankardeva Award' conferred on Bhabendranath Saikia.

1999
- Film and Television Institute, 'Jyoti Chitraban', inaugurated at Guwahati on 17th January.

2000
- Nirupama Phukan awarded with the 'Sahitya Akademi Award for her translation works on 21st February.

2001
- Krishna Deka Raja and Bahniman Bora became the proud Champions in the National Junior Badminton Championship on 16th December.

2002
- Nalinidhar Bhattacharya honoured with the 'Chaganlal Jain Award' on 9th January.

2003
- A tripartite agreement was signed between the centre, the Assam government and the Bodo Liberation Tigers (BLT) at New Delhi for the creation of an autonomous self-governing body, the Bodo Territorial Council (BTC) on February.

2004
- The prestigious USA based organisation. International Fund for Animal Welfare has selected the Forest Minister of Assam Pradyut Bordoloi for the Animal Welfare Politician of the year award for 2004.

2005
- 'Mahakash, Mahasagar Aru Bhupen Hazarika' - a book on critical analysis of music and lyrics of Bhupen Hazarika-authored by Hiranya Kumar Das was released on 5th February, 2005 in New Delhi.

2006
- Debojit Saha of Assam won the prestigious Zee TV's 'Sa Re Ga MaPa' contest held at Mumbai on 24th February 2006 by securing over 2.77 crore votes.
- **On 27th February 2006, the name of the state of Assam was changed to 'Asom'.**
- The Kaziranga National Park in Assam famed added another feather to its cap when it was declared, a tiger reserve under the Project Tiger Scheme in New Delhi on August 9.

- Mr Firoz Ahmed, a wildlife biologist and environmental educator with conservation group *Aaranyak*, was awarded one of the five Wildlife Service Awards given by Sanctuary-ABN AMORO on December 2.

2007
- Purabi Barmudoi, a famous novelist of Assam has been awarded the 'Chaganlal Jain Literary Award' on February 4.

2008
- Donbosco University the first Private University of Assam was inaugurated by Former Chief Minister Tarun Gogoi.

2009
- Eminent artiste Dr Bhupen Hazarika was honoured with the first 'Assam Ratna' award by Government of Assam.

2012
- Sahitya Akademi awardee and famous literary figure of Assam Hiren Bhattacharya passed away on July 4, 2012.
- Sarbananda Sonowal was appointed as the state President of Bharatiya Janata Party (BJP).
- Eminent literary figure of Assam Imran Shah was elected as the new President of Asom Sahitya Sabha.

2013
- Assamese music director Sher Chaudhary passed away.
- The central government has accepted an Assam government proposal for a metro rail project in Guwahati.

2015
- Bus Service had started between Guwahati and Dhaka.

2016
- The Assam Government has granted district status to Majuli a 400 square Kilometer island in the Brahmaputra River, with this it becomes India's first island district.
- The recent census carried out in Kaziranga National Park, Assam has revealed that there was a marginal increase in the population of the one-horned rhinoceros here.
- The Airport Authority of India (AAI) has signed Memorandum of Understanding (MoU) with Assam government for sustainable development of human settlements at villages in Kamrup district
- Assam will mark September 22 as Rhino Day.
- The Union Government has launched new scheme for protection of Majuli Island in Assam from flood and erosion.
- Assam-based ecologist and conservation activist Bibhuti Lahkar has won prestigious 'Heritage Heroes Award'2016 of the International Union for Conservation of Nature (IUCN).
- The Assam Government has launched Rhino horn verification process for verifying rhino horns stored in various treasuries of Assam since 1980.

2017
- The 6th International Tourism Mart (ITM) 2017 was held in Guwahati, Assam.
- The first ever Namami Barak festival was held at Silchar in Assam.
- The Union Government and World Bank have signed $200 million Loan Agreement for Assam Agribusiness and Rural Transformation Project.
- The Prime Minister Narendra Modi has laid the Foundation Stone of the Indian Agricultural Research Institute at Gogamukh in Assam's Dhemaji district located on the Assam-Arunachal Pradesh border.
- Prime Minister Narendra Modi has inaugurated India's longest river bridge – the Dhola-Sadia Bridge in Assam. He has also renamed the bridge as Bhupen Hazarika Bridge.

- Assam Government has launched Chief Minister Samagra Gramya Unnayan Yojana (CMSGUY) to bring about paradigm shift towards holistic development of villages in the state.
- Assam Government rolled out 'Atal-Amrit Abhiyan', a health insurance scheme to provide coverage against several critical illnesses.
- Assam government has launched 'Sustainable Action for Climate Resilient Development in Majuli' (SACReD, Majuli) to make river island Majuli country's first ever Carbon Neutral district by 2020.
- Hailakandi district of Assam has become the first district to pay wages to tea garden workers through individual bank accounts.
- The Union Human Resource Development (HRD) Minister Prakash Javadekar has inaugurated the super computer PARAM ISHAN at IIT Guwahati campus.

2018

- PM Modi inaugurated the Bogibeel Bridge on the birth anniversary of the late Atal Bihari Vajpayee i.e. December 25,2018 which is observed as "Good Governance Day". This 4.9 km-long bridge is the nation's only fully welded bridge and for the first time European codes and welding standards were adhered to and it has a life of about 120 years.
- Government of India and Asian Development Bank (ADB) have signed a loan agreement of $60 million for financing project for renovation, protection and community-based flood risk management activities along the Brahmaputra river in Assam
- United Nations International Children's Emergency Fund (UNICEF) has appointed popular singer Nahid Afrin (17) of Assam as the first 'Youth Advocate' of the northeastern region to fight for child rights. UNICEF engages 'Youth Advocates' to harness their voice as agents of change in society. Nahid had made her playback debut in 2016 Bollywood film 'Akira' starring Sonakshi Sinha in the lead. She received best female playback singer award at the Assam state Film Award 2018.
- Assamese movie 'Village Rockstars' was selected as India's official entry to the Oscars 2019 (91st Academy Awards) under Foreign Language Film category.
- Inland Waterways Authority of India (IWAI) in collaboration with Assam Government has launched new Roll on-Roll off (Ro-Ro) facility connecting Neamati to Manjuli Island in Assam
- Union Cabinet approves New National Institutes Of Design,in Jorhat, Assam.
- Hima Das appointed as Sports Ambassador of Assam
- The Digital North East Vision 2022 was released in Guwahati, Assam by Union Minister for Electronics & Information Technology Ravi Shankar Prasad.
- President Ram Nath Kovind has Assam Witch Hunting (Prohibition, Prevention and Protection) Bill, 2015 passed by State Assembly in August 2015. This law aims to reign in rising incidents of witch hunting cases across the state.
- Numaligarh Refinery Ltd (NRL) in Assam became first oil public sector undertaking (PSU) in India to adopt an online legal compliance system by introducing 'Legatrix'.
- Assam Spring Festival organised at Manas National Park.

23 Multiple Choice Questions

1. **According to the 2011 census, total population of Assam is:**
   (a) 12,868,391
   (b) 26,655, 528
   (c) 2,46,65,528
   (d) 31,205,576
2. **According to 2011 Census, male population of Assam is:**
   (a) 15,939,443
   (b) 1,38,78,591
   (c) 13,777,037
   (d) 1,17,67,337
3. **According to 2011 Census Female population of Assam is:**
   (a) 12,878,491
   (b) 1,18,68,491
   (c) 15,266,133
   (d) 1,38,68,491
4. **Capital of Assam is:**
   (a) Jorhat
   (b) Lakhimpur
   (c) Disapur
   (d) Guwahati
5. **What is the area of Assam?**
   (a) 68,438 sq. km.
   (b) 69,738 sq. km.
   (c) 88,438 sq. km.
   (d) 78,438 sq. km.
6. **How many districts are there in Assam?**
   (a) 34 (b) 35
   (c) 25 (d) 27
7. **Longest river of Assam is:**
   (a) Brahamaputra River
   (b) Barak River
   (c) Dhansiri River
   (d) Kapili River
8. **Which is the main crop of Assam is:**
   (a) Wheat
   (b) Mesta
   (c) Millet
   (d) Rice
9. **Assam University is situated at:**
   (a) Guwahati
   (b) Tinsukia
   (c) Dibrugarh
   (d) Silchar
10. **State animal of Assam is:**
    (a) Elephant
    (b) Rhino
    (c) Tiger
    (d) Buffalo
11. **According to 2011 Census, Urban population in Assam is:**
    (a) 14.10% (b) 11.72%
    (c) 9.72% (d) 10.14%
12. **Assam Legislative Assembly consist of:**

(a) 111 (b) 100
(c) 120 (d) 126

13. In Lok Sabha, total number of Seats reserved for Assam is:
(a) 14 (b) 15
(c) 16 (d) 18

14. The ancient name of Cachar was:
(a) Narayanpur
(b) Daipur
(c) Hidimba
(d) Dhanashree

15. Main tribe of Assam is:
(a) Rabha (b) Miri
(c) Boro (d) Mikir

16. According to 2011 Census, population density in Assam is:
(a) 340 per sq. km.
(b) 397 per sq. km.
(c) 398 per sq. km.
(d) 400 sq. km.

17. In Rajya Sabha, total number of seats reserved for Assam is :
(a) 7 (b) 8
(c) 9 (d) 11

18. 'Bihu' is the important festival of:
(a) Arunachal Pradesh
(b) Assam
(c) Meghalaya
(d) Mizorame

19. According to 2011 Census, Females Literacy Rate in Assam is:
(a) 54.61%
(b) 65.70%
(c) 66.27%
(d) 74.63%

20. According to 2011 Census, Male Literacy Rate in Assam is:
(a) 55.62% (b) 71.81%
(c) 77.85% (d) 71.28%

21. According to the census 2011,Which one of the following districts has largest population?
(a) Dhubri
(b) Kamrup
(c) Nagaon
(d) Barpeta

22. Who was the first Chief Minister of Assam?
(a) Golap Borbora
(b) Gopinath Bordoloi
(c) Tarun Gogoi
(d) Bishnu Ram Madhi

23. State Flower of Assam is :
(a) Foxtail Orchid (Kopou phul)
(b) Lotus
(c) Palash
(d) Siroi Lily

24. Who was not a Chief Minister of Assam in independent India?
(a) Gopinath Bordoloi
(b) Jogendra Nath Hazarika
(c) Keshab Chandra Gogoi
(d) Sir Muhammad Sadulla

25. State bird of Assam is :
(a) White-winged wood duck
(b) House sparrow

(c) Yellow-footed green pigeon
(d) Sarus crane

26. **State Tree of Assam is :**
(a) Sal (b) Mango
(c) Hollong (d) Banyan

27. **In which year, Tocklai Tea Research Centre was established?**
(a) 1910 (b) 1911
(c) 1914 (d) 1915

28. **Lokpriya Gopinath Bordoloi International Airport is situated at :**
(a) Johrat
(b) Guwahati
(c) Silchar
(d) Tezpur

29. **Which of the following is the Largest City in Assam?**
(a) Dibrugarhi
(b) Tinsukia
(c) Guwahat
(d) Silchar

30. **Which one of the following is not an official language of Assam?**
(a) Bengali (b) Hindi
(c) Bodo (d) English

31. **The main river flowing through Assam is :**
(a) Krishna
(b) Ganga
(c) Brahmaputra
(d) Kosi

32. **The Burmese attacked and captured Assam in :**
(a) 1816 (b) 1818
(c) 1821 (d) 1826

33. **Which of the following town is also known as Manchester of Assam?**
(a) Diphu
(b) Digboi
(c) Sualkuchi
(d) Guwahati

34. **Namghosa was written by:**
(a) Madhabdev
(b) Shabnkardev
(c) Madhava Kandali
(d) Both (a) and (b)

35. **The first king of Khen dynasty was :**
(a) Prithu
(b) Bishwa Singha
(c) Bhiga
(d) Bhiru

36. **In which place the first battle fought by Ahom king against the Mughals?**
(a) Bharali
(b) Saraighat
(c) Itakhuli
(d) Jogighopa

37. **Most Important king of Varman dynasty in 7th century was :**
(a) Bhaskar Varman
(b) Chandar Varman
(c) Surya Varman
(d) Harshadeva

38. **Assam is located between**
(a) 82 - 85° E, 24 - 26° N
(b) 90 - 96° E, 24 - 28° N
(c) 92 - 95° E, 25 - 29° N
(d) 93 - 85° E. 23 - 30° N

39. **Who was the first Assamese woman justice of High Court?**

(a) Meera Sarma
(b) Parul Das
(c) Nalinibala Devi
(d) Aaideu Handique

40. 'Noonmati' is famous for
(a) Copper Reserve
(b) Coat Reserve
(c) Oil Refinery
(d) Sugar Refinery

41. Me - Dum - Me - Phi is a famous :
(a) Dance (b) Festival
(c) Food (d) Music

42. Assam is situated on latitude between :
(a) 24° N and 28° N
(b) 30° N and 36° N
(c) 32° N and 36° N
(d) None of these

43. In Assam, homestead garden is locally known as :
(a) Aami
(b) Bari
(c) Kuli
(d) Both (a) and (b)

44. Dispur became the capital of Assam in :
(a) 1969 (b) 1970
(c) 1971 (d) 1973

45. Kaziranga National Park is famous for :
(a) Birds
(b) One Horned Rhino
(c) Elephant
(d) Tiger

46. Which of the following is known as the gateway to the North-Eastern Region?
(a) Silchar
(b) Barpeta
(c) Guwahati
(d) Dispur

47. Ghiyasuddin Auliya associated with
(a) Rangamati Masjid
(b) Panbari Masjid
(c) Poa Mecca of Hazo
(d) Both (a) and (b)

48. The Terracotta industry is located in :
(a) Goalpara
(b) Dhemaji
(c) Dhubri
(d) Karimganj

49. Shiv Dol was constructed during the reign of :
(a) Shiva Singha
(b) Rudra Singha
(c) Purandar Singha
(d) Suhungmung

50. Under the Govt. of India Act 1935, Assam Legislative Assembly was formed in:
(a) 1935 (b) 1936
(c) 1937 (d) 1938

51. The most famous tourist place 'Rang Ghar' was built by-
(a) Rudra Singh
(b) Shankardeva Kalkheshtra
(c) Pramatta Singha
(d) Rajeshwar singha

52. Which is the most important and common festival of Assam?
(a) Bihu (b) Lohri
(c) Onam (d) Pongal

53. **How many National Parks are there in Assam?**
(a) 4
(b) 5
(c) 6
(d) 7

54. **According to 2011 Census, Sex ratio in Assam is:**
(a) 958
(b) 893
(c) 954
(d) 935

55. **According to 2011 census, literacy rate of Assam is:**
(a) 75.3% (b) 70%
(c) 72.19% (d) 60.8%

56. **Name of the first Ahom king was :**
(a) Sudangpha
(b) Subinpha
(c) Sukafa
(d) Suseupha

57. **The oldest cannon inscriptions discovered in Assam belonged to which dynasty?**
(a) Koch
(b) Ahoms
(c) Mughals
(d) British

58. **In 1874, Assam was separated from Bengal and became a separate province with its capital in ....**
(a) Dibrugarh
(b) Guwahati
(c) Shillong
(d) Lakhimpur

59. **....... was a unique creation of Srimanta Sankardeva.**
(a) Katha Gita
(b) Bhakti Ratnavali
(c) Naamghar
(d) Ghar

60. **According to Census 2011, percentage of rural population in Assam is :**
(a) 71.85%
(b) 50.70%
(c) 85.90%
(d) 70.90%

61. **The confluence point of Brahmaputra River is:**
(a) Indian Ocean
(b) Bay of Bengal
(c) Arabian Sea
(d) None of these

62. **Assam State Electricity Board (ASEB) was constituted in :**
(a) 1950
(b) 1958
(c) 1955
(d) 1960

63. **The first Assamese Children's magazine:**
(a) Mouchak
(b) Natun Awiskar
(c) Lora Bandhu
(d) Safura

64. **Who was the first Assamese author to receive Jnanpith Award?**
(a) Nilmani Phookan
(b) Pushpalata Das
(c) Indira Goswami
(d) Dr Birendra Kumare Bhattacharya

65. **'Gagang' the famous musical instrument of Assam is made up of-**

(a) Teakwood
(b) buffalo horn
(c) bamboo
(d) cane

66. Which of the following Ahom kings planned to invasion of Bengal?
(a) Shiva Singha
(b) Rudra Singha
(c) Suhungmung
(d) Gadadhar Singha

67. Nehru Stadium of Assam was built in :
(a) 1960 (b) 1962
(c) 1963 (d) 1965

68. Sualkuchi is famous for:
(a) Cotton Industry
(b) Iron Industry
(c) Leather Industry
(d) Silk Industry

69. Capital of Ahom Kingdom was:
(a) Guwahati
(b) Jorhat
(c) Sibsagar
(d) Shillong

70. How many Sub-divisions are there in Assam?
(a) 28 (b) 38
(c) 49 (d) 58

71. When was National Games held in Assam?
(a) 2001 (b) 2005
(c) 2007 (d) 2011

72. Srimanta Sankaradeva started Neo-Vaishnava movement in Assam in :
(a) 12th century
(b) 13th century
(c) 14th century
(d) 15th century

73. Chinese traveller Hiuen Tsang Visited Assam in the :
(a) 6th century
(b) 7th century
(c) 8th century
(d) 9th century

74. Which of the following is state drink of Assam?
(a) Coffee
(b) Milk
(c) Tea
(d) Both (a) and (c)

75. The Guwahati Tea Auction Centre was established in the year :
(a) 1960 (b) 1965
(c) 1970 (d) 1975

76. Who was the first Assamese Chief Justice in Supreme Court of India?
(a) Ranjan Kumar Gogoi
(b) Mahindra Mohan Choudhary
(c) Parbati Kumar Goswami
(d) Haliram Deka

77. Nameri National Park is located in :
(a) Dibrugarh district
(b) Tinsukia district
(c) Lakhimpur district
(d) Sonitpur district

78. The first newspaper of Assam (North-East) 'Arunodoi' was published in the year:
(a) 1844
(b) 1846
(c) 1850
(d) 1890

79. Who was Sir Akbar Hydari?
(a) Chief Justice of High Court
(b) Governor of Assam
(c) Election Commissioner of India
(d) Speaker of Assam Legislative Assembly

80. The first tea company established in Assam was :
(a) Assam-Bengal Tea Company
(b) Assam Company
(c) Jorhat Tea Company
(d) None of these

81. What was the ancient name of Assam mentioned in Ramayana and Mahabharta ?
(a) Pragiyotishpura
(b) Kamrup
(c) Indraprastha
(d) Patliputra

82. Who was the first and only lady became the Chief Minister of Assam till now?
(a) Anowara Taimur
(b) Nalinbala Devi
(c) Rani Narah
(d) Parul Das

83. Who is the only Assamese President of Indian National Congress?
(a) Fakhruddin Ali Ahmed
(b) Deva Kanta Barua
(c) Navakanta Barua
(d) Harishankar Brahma

84. 'Khorahi' in Assamese means:
(a) Small basket
(b) Turban
(c) Trunk
(d) Mat

85. A natural golden coloured silk produced in Assam is named?
(a) Palka (b) Raw
(c) Sualki (d) Muga

86. Navagraha Temple is situated in :
(a) Digboi (b) Namrup
(c) Silchar (d) Guwahati

87. Varman Dynasty in Assam began with :
(a) Awanthi Varman
(b) Kamarupak
(c) Pushya Varman
(d) Suhungmung

88. At which of the following places, the River Subansiri completely enters into Assam?
(a) Dhemaji
(b) Gerukamukh
(c) Lakhimpur
(d) Bangpari

89. Which language is used by Sankardeva to written first Borgeet?
(a) Assamese
(b) Brajavali
(c) Sanskrit
(d) All of the above

90. The book 'India Against Itself' was written by-
(a) Hem Baruah
(b) Dimbeswar Neog
(c) Sanjib Baruah
(d) Birinchi Kumar Baruah

91. Which one of the following places is the confluence of three highly

revered pilgrimage for the Hindu,Muslim and Biddhist?

(a) Hajo
(b) Barpeta
(c) Kareng GHar
(d) Siva Dol

92. The Wildlife Sanctuary of Assam boasts of the golden langur is:

(a) Hollon Gapar
(b) Pobitora
(c) Borail
(d) Chakrashila

93. The area of Kaziranga National Park is approximately:

(a) 520 sq. km
(b) 340 sq. km
(c) 858 sq. km
(d) 200 sq. km

94. Eri,Muga and Pat are different types of-

(a) Assam Tea
(b) Assam Fish
(c) Assam Silk
(d) All of the above

95. Assam state enjoys-

(a) hot climate
(b) cold climate
(c) warm climate
(d) tropical climate

96. Terai zone is situated at Assam's

(a) East zone
(b) West zone
(c) South zone
(d) North zone

97. Name the famous Shiva Temple located on the Peacock Island in the middle of the Brahmaputra river in Guwahati-

(a) Umananda
(b) Kamakhya
(c) Shiv Dol
(d) Madan Kamdeva

98. Where is the famous Joysagar lake located - it is one of the largest man made lakes in India?

(a) Jorhat
(b) Goalpara
(c) Sivasagar
(d) Dibrugarh

99. The Assam Sahitya Sabha was founded in-

(a) 1911 (b) 1913
(c) 1916 (d) 1917

100. The first Assamese film 'Joymoti' was released in the year-

(a) 1930 (b) 1935
(c) 1915 (d) 1922

101. Guwahati University was established in the year–

(a) 1935 (b) 1942
(c) 1944 (d) 1948

102. The first martyr of 1942 Revolution in Assam was :

(a) Jyoti Prasad Agarwala
(b) Kushal Konwar
(c) Kanaklata Barua
(d) Muhammed Saadulah

103. In which year Gopinath Bordoloi was arrested due to active participation in the Non-co-operation movement?

(a) 1915 (b) 1919
(c) 1920 (d) 1922

104. The first One day International Cricket (ODI) match in Assam was played in:

(a) 1980 (b) 1981
(c) 1982 (d) 1983

105. According to area which is the biggest district in Assam?

(a) Tinsukia
(b) Kabri Auglong
(c) Golaghat
(d) Nagaon

Answers

1.	(d)	**2.**	(a)	**3.**	(c)	**4.**	(c)	**5.**	(d)
6.	(b)	**7.**	(a)	**8.**	(d)	**9.**	(d)	**10.**	(b)
11.	(a)	**12.**	(d)	**13.**	(a)	**14.**	(c)	**15.**	(c)
16.	(c)	**17.**	(a)	**18.**	(b)	**19.**	(c)	**20.**	(c)
21.	(c)	**22.**	(b)	**23.**	(a)	**24.**	(d)	**25.**	(a)
26.	(c)	**27.**	(b)	**28.**	(b)	**29.**	(c)	**30.**	(d)
31.	(c)	**32.**	(c)	**33.**	(c)	**34.**	(a)	**35.**	(a)
36.	(c)	**37.**	(a)	**38.**	(b)	**39.**	(a)	**40.**	(c)
41.	(b)	**42.**	(a)	**43.**	(b)	**44.**	(d)	**45.**	(b)
46.	(c)	**47.**	(c)	**48.**	(c)	**49.**	(a)	**50.**	(c)
51.	(c)	**52.**	(a)	**53.**	(b)	**54.**	(a)	**55.**	(c)
56.	(c)	**57.**	(a)	**58.**	(c)	**59.**	(c)	**60.**	(c)
61.	(b)	**62.**	(b)	**63.**	(c)	**64.**	(d)	**65.**	(c)
66.	(b)	**67.**	(b)	**68.**	(d)	**69.**	(c)	**70.**	(d)
71.	(c)	**72.**	(d)	**73.**	(b)	**74.**	(c)	**75.**	(c)
76.	(c)	**77.**	(d)	**78.**	(b)	**79.**	(a)	**80.**	(b)
81.	(a)	**82.**	(a)	**83.**	(b)	**84.**	(a)	**85.**	(d)
86.	(d)	**87.**	(c)	**88.**	(b)	**89.**	(b)	**90.**	(c)
91.	(a)	**92.**	(d)	**93.**	(c)	**94.**	(c)	**95.**	(d)
96.	(a)	**97.**	(a)	**98.**	(c)	**99.**	(d)	**100.**	(b)
101.	(d)	**102.**	(c)	**103.**	(d)	**104.**	(d)	**105.**	(b)

24 What and Where

Agriculture College	:	Jorhat, Biswanath Chariali
Cement Factory	:	Bokajan
Match Factory		Dhubri
Sugar Mills	:	Baruuabamun Gaon, Chargoal (Cachar), Kampur
Aluminium Industries	:	Tinsukia, Nalbari, Bongaigaon, Amingaon
Railway Junctions	:	Lumding, Tinsukia, Simaluguri, Mariani, Rangia, Fakiragram, Badarpur, Farkating, Chaparmukh, North Rangapara etc.
Airports	:	Borjhar (Guwahati), Rawriah (Jorhat), Saloni (Tezpur), Mohanbari (Dibrugarh), Lilabari (North Lakhimpur), Kumbhirgram (Silchar)
Oil Refineries	:	Digboi, Noonmati (Guwahati), Bongaigaon, Numaligarh
Petrochemical Projects	:	Namrup, Bongaigaon
Fertilizer Factory	:	Namrup (Brahmaputra Valley Fertilizer Corporation Ltd.)
Paper Mills	:	Jagiroad, Panchagram
Brahmaputra Bridges	:	Saraighat (Guwahati-Amingaon), Kolia Bhomora (Tezpur),Naranarayan Setu (Jogighopa-Pancharatna), Bogibeel Bridge (Expected completion in 2017)
National Park	:	Kaziranga National Park, Manas National Park, Nameri National Park, Dibru-Saikhowa National Park, Orang National Park

Forest Reserve and Sanctuary	:	Sonai-Rupai, Pobitara, Pabhoi, Laokhowa, Garampani, Bomadi
Tiger Project	:	Manas Tiger Project, Nameri Tiger Project
Largest River Island	:	Majuli (Area 880 sq.km)
Smallest River Island	:	Umananda (Guwahati)
Coal Field	:	Dilli-Joypur. Makum
Oil Field	:	Digboi, Naharkatia, Hoogrijan, Moran, Lakua,Galeki, Rudrasagaretc
Hot Spring	:	Garampani (Golaghat)
China Clay	:	Karbi Anglong
Ayurved College	:	Guwhati
Homeopathic Colleges	:	Guwhati, Jorhat
Fishery College	:	Raha (Nagaon)
Veterinary College	:	Khanapara (Guwahatt)
Regional Engineering College	:	Silchar
Polytechnics	:	Guwahati, Lahowal (Dibrugarh), Diphu, Silchar,Nagaon, Golaghat
Industrial Training Institutes	:	Jorhat, Tinsukia, Guwahati, Tezpur, Barpeta, Bongaigaon, Goalpara etc.
Sainik School	:	Momoi (Goalpara)
Sanskrit Colleges	:	Guwahati, Nalbari
Mental Hospital	:	Tezpur
Regional Research Laboratory	:	Jorhat
State Zoo	:	Guwahati
State Museum	:	Guwhati
Tea Research Centre	:	Jorhat
Planetarium	:	Guwahati
Forest Research Centre	:	Jorhat
Plywood Factories	:	Margherita, Tinsukia, Mariani